Otherness and Pathology:

The Fragmented Self and Madness in Contemporary African Fiction

**Andrew Nyongesa,
Justus Makokha,
Gaita Murimi**

Edited by Tendai R. Mwanaka

Mwanaka Media and Publishing Pvt Ltd,
Chitungwiza Zimbabwe
*
Creativity, Wisdom and Beauty

Publisher: *Mmap*
Mwanaka Media and Publishing Pvt Ltd
24 Svosve Road, Zengeza 1
Chitungwiza Zimbabwe
mwanaka@yahoo.com
mwanaka13@gmail.com
https://www.mmapublishing.org
www.africanbookscollective.com/publishers/mwanaka-media-and-publishing
https://facebook.com/MwanakaMediaAndPublishing/

Distributed in and outside N. America by African Books Collective
orders@africanbookscollective.com
www.africanbookscollective.com

ISBN: 978-1-77925-578-5
EAN: 9781779255785

©Andrew Nyongesa, Justus Makokha, Gaita Murimi 2021

All rights reserved.
No part of this book may be reproduced or transmitted in any form or by any means, mechanical or electronic, including photocopying and recording, or be stored in any information storage or retrieval system, without written permission from the publisher

DISCLAIMER
All views expressed in this publication are those of the author and do not necessarily reflect the views of *Mmap*.

Table of Contents
Introduction 1
1.1 Otherness and Madness: Psychological and Post-colonial Reading of Selected Works of African Fiction 6
Chapter One 10
Otherness and the fragmented Self in Contemporary African Fiction 10
The Non-Self in Alex la Guma's *A Walk in the Night* 11
Otherness and the Fragmented Selves in La Guma's *A Walk in the Night* 15
The Non-self Self and the Mental: the Body as the Other in *A Walk in the Night* 21
Conclusion 25
1.2 26
The Shattered Self and Wanner's *London, Cape Town, Joburg* 26

Suicide and the Fragmented Self and Farah's *Close Sesame* 38

Annihilation of the other Self: Suicide and the Detestable "other" in Self 42

Conclusion 50
Chapter Two 51
Fragmented Natures in Selected works of African Drama 51
Introduction 51
Othering and the Fragmented Self in John Ruganda's *Shreds of Tenderness* 52
Otherness and the Fragmented characters in *Shreds of Tenderness* 53
Political Otherness and the Fragmented Self: Shattered and Multiple Selves 59
Othering and the Fragmented Self: Ideological Relegation and Pathology in David Mulwa's *Inheritance* 67

Age Othering and Pathology: Fragmented Antagonist in Mulwa's *Inheritance* 69
Political Othering and the Shattered Self: Disorders of the Self at the Marginal Space 76
Conclusion 83
Chapter Three 84
Otherness and Madness in African Fiction 84
Introduction 84
Gender Othering and Schizophrenia in Farah's *Gifts* and El Saadawi's *God Dies by the Nile* 86
Gender Othering and Pathology: multiple Selves and Madness in *Gifts* and *God Dies by the Nile* 89
Conclusion 99
Madness and the Other in Farah's *Close Sesame* and Matar's *The Return* 100
3.3 Political Otherness and Psychopathy in *Close Sesame* and *The Return* 104
3.4 Racial Otherness and Pathology in *The Return* and *Close Sesame* 122
Conclusion 129
Chapter Four 130
Otherness and Madness in African Drama 130
Introduction 130
Political Otherness and Psychopathy in Three Works of Drama 131
Othering Conditions and Pathology: Schizophrenic Characters in the Three Selected Plays 132
Conclusion 144
Chapter Five 145
SUMMARY AND CONCLUSIONS 145
Works Cited 148

Introduction

If animals and things looked the same, if all people acted and behaved the same way; the world would be the ugliest and life most boring to live. Difference and variety constitute beauty and the rainbow exemplifies the splendour of dissimilarity. Like the rainbow, the concept of difference is a fact we cannot deny because everyone with eyes that see can see it. John Stuart Mill expresses preference for appreciation of difference and diversity. He exhorts society to abandon imitation and sameness and pursue originality as the praxis of moral development (284). For Mill, difference should be appreciated as a thing of value, a sign of genius rather than a vice to be tolerated in a society. In our world, however, difference is scorned at and stigmatized. Those who do not look or behave like the majority of the populace are relegated through a process called othering. Jean F. Staszak defines othering as the inability to see people who are different as part of one's community. They become "the other" because they do not look or behave like "us" (2). The dominant community is unable to see similarity between *self* and the Other.

The failure of society to embrace difference turns it to otherness- the quality of being fundamentally unusual, somewhat undesirable. Otherness is followed by separation from the rest of the community. Staszak observes that otherness is due less to difference of the Other than the point of view and the discourse of the person who perceives the Other as such (2). Attitude takes centre stage in creation of otherness to turn sex difference into gender otherness or ethnic difference to ethnic otherness (ethnocentrism). The difference, which is real or imagined is exaggerated and stigmatized as a foundation for discrimination.

The process of othering entails assigning a group, an individual the role of the Other and establishing one's identity in a binary opposition to the Other. It begins when the *self* identifies differences of class, ethnicity, age, race, sex, ideology and stigmatizes them. For example, when colonialists referred to Africans as "savages", "barbarians" or "natives," they were simply asserting otherness as the pinnacle of their colonial administration. Frantz Fanon observes, "[c]olonialism is a systematised negation of the Other, a frenzied attempt to deny the other any attribute of humanity..." (*The Wretched of the Earth*, 182). Fanon suggests that othering denies the Other any hold on sameness, for instance reason, dignity, love, pride and any claim to human rights. Richard Rorty asserts, "[e]verything turns on who counts as a fellow human, as a rational agent in the only relevant sense- the sense in which rational agency is synonymous with membership of our moral community" (124). Rorty probably means that one is only treated as a human being if he or she is a member of the social class, ethnic group, racial community, religious group, gender community, agegroup or political party. The rest are strangers to be treated with utter contempt.

The process of othering may be triggered by an encounter of cultures that have no previous contact. Samuel Huntington observes that civilizations clash because the differences among them are not only real but basic (25). Different cultures or civilisations have different views on relations between God and man, the individual and the group. The differences precipitate othering, which has devastating physical and psychological consequences on the Other. The European conquest and near annihilation of Ameri-Indians (native Americans) in the United States is but one illustration and colonial oppression in Africa, another.

Levi Strauss observes that humankind has tended to regard basic differences as "something abnormal or outrageous" (11). People will use expletives like "barbarous habits", "ought not to be allowed," "not what we do" to reject any moral, religious, social ideas, which differ from what they know. Strauss expounds that ancient Europeans covered anything not Greco-Roman by the term "Barbarian". Later, it was changed to "savage", which is a reference to a brutish way of life as opposed to human civilization (11). However, a critical look at it reveals a refusal to admit the fact of cultural diversity or difference. Anything that does not conform to the culture the individual lives is denied the name "culture" and relegated to the realm of nature. Ideally, humanity entails all forms of human species regardless of race, ethnicity, class or creed. Strauss observes that this came into being very late in history and is by no means widespread. He notes:

> Humanity is confined to the borders of the tribe, the linguistic group or even some instances to the village. So that many so called primitive peoples describe themselves "the men", "the good," the excellent, the well achieved implying that the other groups are "the bad", "the wicked," "ground monkeys" (12).

Strauss suggests that othering reduces human beings to nothing by virtue of their diversity. If they are men, women are not human, if they are Socialists then Nationalists are "ground monkeys," if they are adults, children are "bad" and if they are Somalis, Ethiopians are "wicked". Since the *self* cannot agree with the Other, the former erects strong boundaries and special institutions in which they are kept in isolation.

The physical alienation of the Other suggests that there possibly exists a nexus between otherness and alienation. Before interrogating the connection, let us define alienation. The basic meaning of alienation is being cut off from society, family, others and from one's true self. Encyclopaedia Britannica defines alienation as "a state of feeling estranged or separated from one's milieu of work, products or self". Sidney Finkelstein defines alienation as a psychological phenomenon, "an internal conflict, a hostility felt towards something seemingly outside oneself, which is linked to oneself, a barrier erected which is actually no defense but an impoverishment of oneself," (7). These definitions imply that there is alienation in relation to the self and alienation in relation to the Other.

Analyses of Frantz Kafka's diaries demonstrate the most likely attributes expected of a victim of the fragmented self. Kafka was a German novelist whose traumatic experiences fragmented his self. In one of the diaries he writes:

> Up and down in Mr. H's yard, a dog puts his paw on the tip of my foot and I shake. Children, chicken here and there adults; a children's nurse, occasionally leaning on the railing of the *pawlatche* (balcony) or hiding behind a door, her eye on me. Under her eyes, I do not know just what I am, whether indifferent or embarrassed, young or old, impudent or devoted…animal lover or man of affairs, Jew or Christian. (Kafka, 79)

Kafka observes the children's nurse, and a dog but he cannot locate where his self fits in. In psychological terms, Kafka has a fractured view of himself because not one image of "self" satisfies him. There are so many selves available to him: Jew or Christian, animal lover or man of affairs… he is at loss. Kafka's diaries lead us to the definition of the fragmented self as a soul in turmoil; self-doubt, in severe depression; a fractured person seeking for some regular pattern in the little, broken life. For Richard Gray, such a fragmented life is in constant search for all elusive wholeness (264). Kafka's diaries suggest the following as features of the fragmented:

The victim suffers from depression and hopelessness. Most parts of the diary reveal symptoms of depression such as self-doubt, self-criticism, and self-hatred; sense of panic, desire to hide oneself, physical pain and insomnia. He writes, "[s]leepless night. The third in a row…I feel myself rejected by sleep… towards morning, I sigh into my pillow because this night all hope is gone" (60). The lack of sleep is attributed to mental disturbance and extreme tension as a result of mental distress.

Furthermore, the victim suffers from alienation. It is estrangement and feeling of being an outsider. In his diary on 21st August 1913, he reveals that he had not spoken more than twenty words a day to his parents the previous year and does not speak to his sisters and brothers-in-law and not because he has anything against them. The reason he gives is:

> I have not the slightest thing to talk to them about. Everything that is not literature bores me and I hate it. I lack all aptitude for family life except at best as an observer. I have no family feeling and visitors make me almost feel as though I were maliciously being attacked. (231)

Kafka's overbearing father possibly alienated him and he took to writing as a self-defence mechanism. His sad history of intermittent bouts of Tuberculosis and consumption were traumatic experiences that caused his self-fragmentation. Ronald Laing refers to victims of the fragmented self as schizoids- individuals whose personality is split in two ways: A rend in his relationship with the world and a break in his relationship with himself (17). Kafka probably fits this description since he had difficulty in forming relationships with the opposite sex and would not get married throughout his life. His focus on writing suggests that the self was exclusively concerned with mental processes.

Otherness and Madness: Psychological and Post-colonial Reading of Selected Works of African Fiction

Some studies in madness have tended to associate the anomaly with personal weaknesses. Donald Roberts avers that during the Augustan period in Europe, mad people were mistreated because they were perceived as weak individuals that easily breakdown by reason of their fear (13). Roberts contends that madness does not solely arise from hereditary conditions, but the cultural landscape. This book extends Roberts argument that cultural aspects such as strands of otherness drive individuals to madness with evidence from selected works of African fiction.

Post-colonial scholars have demonstrated how the political arm of society can invent otherness and drive the subjects to madness. Through a blend of racial and political othering, the cultural setting becomes very toxic on the self of the oppressed. In the chapter, "Concerning violence," Fanon describes the colonial world as "defined by otherness," (39), a binary world of the settler on the one hand and the native on the other. The settler lives behind fenced walls and the native exploited by constantly working on his farms. The native's world is delineated by congestion and stagnation: [t]he native town is hungry town, starved of bread, of meat, of shoes, of coal, of light; a town on its knees, a town wallowing in mire," (39). The constant deprivation in the colonized's town is juxtaposed to the lofty homes of the settler's behind the fenced walls. Otherized by the system to live in indigence, the native becomes, "[a]n envious man, bitter and the settler knows this well when they meet," (39). Laing refers to the bitterness brought out in this excerpt as the fragmented self; the African's self is depressed because of deliberate othering.

Fanon contends that the violence that erupts in Africa during the struggle for independence cannot be solely tied to class struggle as Marxists claim because, "[i]n the colonies, the economic substructure is also superstructure- you are rich because you are white, you are white because you are rich," (40). In other words, the othering in the colonies is based on race rather than class. It is the race that determines the social class in colonial Africa; it is the qualification that determines the job one takes and attribute that gauges one's promotion. The value of one's culture is gauged by the race and so white people have a superior and Africans, inferior culture in a colonial setting. Fanon writes:

> The customs of the colonized people, their traditions, their myths- are the very sign of that poverty of spirit and of their constitutional depravity. That is why we must put DDT, which destroys parasites. (41)

African's culture is described as destitute of value and testifies of the very intellectual hollowness (constitutional depravity) and like "parasites" or "pests" it should be sprayed with pesticides for total annihilation. The colonizer therefore strives to change the colonized by introducing a new way of life in spite of the genetic mediocrity ascribed to the colonized. In most colonial entities, Africans were perceived as lazy and fools by heredity rather than environment. Fanon writes, "[t]he cerebral structure of the North African are responsible both for the native's laziness, for his intellectual and social inaptitude and for his almost animal impulsivity," (302). The African brain "lacks integration of the frontal lobes," which makes him naturally lazy, foolish with propensity for crimes and rape. These theories informed the callousness with which colonialism was executed to "disrupt the cultural life" of the colonized through "negation of national reality…banishment of natives and their customs" (235) which dented the self-esteem of the colonized. In the last chapter, "The Colonial War and Mental Disorders," Fanon summarises his views on colonialism as, "[a] systematised negation of the other, a frenzied attempt to deny the other any attribute of humanity...which if left unchallenged by armed resistance, the colonized's defenses collapse and many of them end up in psychiatric institutions," (250). Fanon adds that a stream of symptoms of madness ensues as "sequels of the oppression" (250). He gives examples of the colonized who lose their mental health after clash with the colonizer. There is a case of an Algerian man who survives a massacre when French soldiers shoot twenty nine Algerians. He is so traumatized by the ordeal that he picks a gun and threatens to shoot everyone saying that they are spies of French soldiers (252). . As a consequence, Fanon gives us examples of many Africans who ran mad in Algeria. A man who survives a massacre when the French soldiers shoot twenty nine African soldiers picks a gun and wants to shoot everyone saying that everyone present is a French soldier and should be killed (191).

Fanon's ideas offer a basis of analysis in this study as they expound the concept of othering as demonstrated through colonialism. Colonial oppression is premised on racial and political otherness, which fragments the self of the Africans. Fanon's observation that the "colonized's defenses collapse" (250) under the onslought of oppression is a reference to madness, a major concept of analysis in this study.

Whereas Fanon's focus is racial and political otherness, this study extends it to class otherness, where social class differences are stigmatized, gender otherness, which entails stigmatization of sex differences to relegate men or women; age otherness where adults stigmatize children and downgrade them; ethnic otherness—stereotyping of a certain race or ethnic group by the dominant majority; ideology, where a group is relegated because of what they believe and culture, which involves discrimination based on differences in the way of life.

8

In this book, we interrogate the nexus between otherness and psychological anomalies such as the fragmented self and madness in selected works of African fiction. The works under study include Hisham Matar's *The Return*, Nuruddin Farah's *Gifts* and *Close Sesame*; David Mulwa's *Inheritance*, John Ruganda's *Shreds of Tenderness* and Francis Imbuga's *Betrayal in the City;* Alex La Guma's *A Walk in the Night* and Zukiswa Wanner's *London, Cape Town, Joburg*. Using postcolonial theory, the author extends the notion that madness arises from without rather than within characters and brings new evidence that when characters exist in settings in which they are stigmatized in whichever way, their psyches collapse and they experience psychological anomalies. Stigmatization takes the form of ethnicity- stereotyping of a certain race or ethnic group by the dominant majority and ideology, where a group is relegated because of what they believe in.

Chapter One

Otherness and the Fragmented Self in Contemporary African Fiction

1.1 The Non-Self in Alex la Guma's *A Walk in the Night*

> La Guma's descriptive style is justifiable in terms of "socialist realist" aesthetic that gives vital expression to the materialist premise informing his Marxist view of the human condition.
>
> *Gareth Cornwell*

Many literary critics have analysed La Guma's works through Marxist lenses possibly because of his tendency to represent the underdog with amazing attention to detail. The depiction of abjection in the marginalized groups in his fiction has been summarized to class oppression and hastily linked to the Marxist template and hence is the subject of Gareth Cornwell's study. In his perspective, La Guma's attention to detail betrays the Marxist social realism (i) through which he looks at the socially stratified society of South Africa and his description of the indigence among the marginalized portrays the Marxist focus on the material condition of humanity. Jabulani J. T Mkhize underscores Cornwell's view when he asserts that La Guma's intention of writing *A Walk in the Night* is to provide a broader account of the plight of the proletariat in District Six (94). He adds that la Guma's assertion in one of the interviews that a gangster is created by society implies that he is informed by Marxist economic determinism (95). In other words, the gangster is a product of socio economic forces that compel them to that condition to balance the wealth between the rival classes.

As much as Marxist criticism stands out as a dominant voice in the analysis of La Guma's fiction, it will be absurd to declare it as the sole perspective through which to analyse the writer's subjects and intention. In one of his interviews, La Guma observes that his emphasis is on depiction of the realities of his South Africans. He asserts "African literature should be assessed in terms of African realities" (Mkhize, 61). Will it be prudent to interpret "African realities" as solely material? For psychological critics, "realities" entail "the unconscious," which is an essential component of the self. Post-colonial scholars view the reality as "tension" between the dominant and marginalized group (Ashcroft Bill and Colleagues, 3) at diverse levels including age, gender, race and ethnicity. Class is just one of these realities and for Frantz Fanon, these strands of otherness result in psychic collapse (182) and cause myriad psychological problems. Richard Gray and colleagues single out the fragmented self as a psychological problem that stems from traumatic experiences such as otherness. He defines it as a self in turmoil; self-doubt, in severe depression; a fractured person seeking for some regular pattern in the little, broken life (264). To underscore the postcolonial conversation, Anders Breidlid looks at marginalized selves as "non-selves" that assert themselves through hybridity. Using the example of Michael Adonis, he writes:

> As a subaltern, Michael Adonis speaks through silences, signalling a mood resistant to Apartheid. He is in a liminal space where he "accepts" and "resists," at the same time. He exposes a hybrid self which necessarily is unstable, fragmented, agonized and in a fluid state. (110)

Breidlid implies that marginalized groups are so shattered by otherness that when they come in contact with agents of the self, they outwardly "accept" orders but mentally "resist" them. Laing defines such characters as schizoids as they experience a split between their bodies and mind and only fit for operations that are purely mental (67-73). The double identity of two equally opposed realities affects their mental health as underscored by Fanon, Gray and Laing.

This subchapter rejects emphasis on Marxist interpretation in La Guma's work and focuses on the psychological effects of otherness on marginalized characters. Using post-colonial and psychological criticism, the subsection demonstrates how aspects of otherness like racial, age, gender and class otherness result in strains of the fragmented self like depression, and unembodied self in La Guma's *A Walk in the Night*. The ideas of Frantz Fanon and Ronald Liang will form a theoretical basis of interpretation.

Synopsis of La Guma's *A Walk in the Night*

A Walk in the Night is a harrowing tale of the psychological consequences of otherness on Michael Adonis and fellow colored characters in District Six in Cape Town. The story has a time span of approximately twelve hours when Michael loiters on Hanover Street at night after being sacked by his white employer. The boss sacks Michael because he has instituted strict working conditions for black workers; he laments anytime they take a break to go for short call (4). Michael gets annoyed by the boss' draconian rules and is dismissed. He leaves the factory and as he wanders in town as vagabonds do, his psyche begins the process of disintegration. Anger, hatred for the whites and self-pity set in as he loiters like many other coloured and black vagrants in District Six. Shattered by otherized conditions, most youth and adults that Michael meets this night across races are so psychologically wrecked that they cannot face the world in a sober frame of mind. They are either alcoholics or substance abusers, which gives a hint into their fragmented natures. First is Willieboy who is addicted to phantasy and wine and confesses that owing to the racist policies in work places, he does not work (4). Foxy and the boy with a scar on his face abuse drugs and fancy violence to drown their sorrows (6). The many pubs that Michael finds as he loiters in the street symbolize the fragmented selves in the novella. He also comes across many street children like Bigger, a chain smoker (24). When he reaches his residence, Michael comes across Uncle Doughty, a former actor that is so depressed that he has given his life to alcoholism. He is described as "deserted, abandoned ruin; destroyed by alcohol or something neither he nor Michael Adonis" (25) could not tell. Out of his anger at the white boss, Michael starts a scuffle and strikes Uncle Doughty dead. To anger, Michael adds fear and guilt as he loiters in Hanover Street. La Guma introduces other characters like Police Constable Raalt, Franky Lorenzo and Joe that also are fragmented by strands of otherness to exhibit anger, self-pity and depression. Raalt's, like Michael's racial hate is in fact a mask that conceals the conflict between him and the wife. The actual conflicts in Raalt, Michael and others are internal, but characters fail to resolve them and opt for the race hood. Raalt shoots Willieboy casting aspersions on his race yet in reality he is trying to resolve the conflict with his apparently superior wife (62). Michael decides to join gangsters against Joe's advice with the misleading thought that through violence he will resolve his fragmented state of anger, guilt and fear. Joe stands out as symbol of hope and determination in the face of otherizing conditions. He resolves to maintain mental and moral sanity in spite of the class and racial otherness in District Six.

Otherness and the Fragmented Selves in La Guma's *A Walk in the Night*

The Fragmented self in La Guma's novella first takes the trajectory of what Heinz Kohut and Earnest Wolf refer to as the under stimulated self, defined as a disorder in which characters lack vitality and experience themselves as boring, apathetic and are experienced by others the same way (418). Desperate for happiness, characters stimulate themselves by addictive promiscuous activities, perversions, gambling, drug and alcohol induced excitement and lifestyle characterized by hyper sociability. This section will investigate whether the characters that experience the anomaly are exposed to a strand of otherness.

The prime mover, Michael Adonis resorts to smoking and alcoholism throughout his journey in Hanover Street. As the sun sets, he joins the vagabonds on the street loitering to no specific place. He enters the pub and is described as "a centre of the lost and despairing" (12). Many coloured people have gathered here to drink and find some excitement that they would never have in a racially hostile environment. Michael comes across so many black youth around the pub that are addicted to hard drugs (13). Bigger for example smokes all the time and he claims he has so many troubles (24). When Michael reaches his house, he meets Uncle Doughty and although he is a white man, he is an alcoholic. In a melancholy description of himself, Uncle Doughty says, "[h]ere I am and nobody to look after an old man," (26). Incessant depression is the probable cause of his alcoholism. He reveals that his wife passed on and that he has lived alone hence forth. Constable Raalt, another white person, smokes (29) and hurls expletives at blacks in District Six. Even while taking Willieboy for treatment after he shoots him, Raalt orders the driver to stop to buy cigarettes (77). Willieboy is another coloured character addicted to both wine and music; he refuses to confront realities of life. As the story begins, he tells Michael that he will never work and so spends his time wining and dancing in pubs (4). Benard Hart observes that obsession with music and drama is a psychological problem. He writes:

> The patient has immersed himself in his imaginary world even more completely and efficiently. The phantasy created by his own mind acquires the tang of actual reality; he believes that he is the conquering hero or multi-millionaire and that the pleasant pictures he once imagined have become facts of life. He has crossed the barrier which separates the normal man's day-dreams from the dreams that accompany sleep and the creations of an idle fancy have become the delusions of insanity. (160)

Hart's description is not just the plight of Willieboy, but of most the aforementioned characters that opt for substance abuse to escape the realities of life. Willieboy even pleads with Miss Gipsy to get wine on credit to bolster his phantasy world (50). As Michael complains about being sacked, Willieboy pays for a new song at the Juke box because as Hart says, "the creations of an idle fancy have become the delusions of insanity" (160). Similarly, Michael, Raalt and Uncle Doughty conceal their traumatic experiences in the phantasy world of smoking, alcoholism and drama. Uncle Doughty was an actor; he tells Michael how he toured Great Britain, South Africa and Australia (25). He demonstrates his artistic talent by quoting Shakespearean lines, "I am thy father's spirit; doomed for a certain term to walk the night," (27). In Hart's perspective, Doughty's obsession with drama is "immersion in the imaginary world" to escape realities of life.

In Fanon's view, it is exposure to otherness that results in psychological anomalies such as the under stimulated self. Michael's addiction to smoking and wine possibly stems from racial stigmatization at the work place. As a coloured person, the white master expects him to work non-stop because he is the other while whites are the self. Michael tells Willieboy, "[e]verytime a man goes to the piss house, he (boss) starts moaning," (4). The black workers have no right to complain and so he is fired. The ensuing trauma is so much to handle without wine and smoking. Uncle Doughty possibly confronts both racial, age and class otherness. The narrator says, "[d]eserted abandoned ruin, destroyed by alcohol and something neither he nor Michael Adonis understood," (25). The unknown thing is a possible reference to the "unconscious," which causes psychological conflicts. In the same way, Uncle Doughty possibly disliked racial otherness that apartheid propagated and this is evident through his decision to marry a coloured wife and live in District Six (26). He was possibly rejected by his white friends and relatives and the blacks in the same measure and his wife's demise worsened the loneliness. Ian Goldin observes "[t]he mixed residential areas of Cape Town were according to the nationalist parliamentarians the deathbed of the European race," (170). White men that married across race like Uncle Doughty were adversaries of the ruling nationalist party as they acted in league with liberal forces that were perceived as eradicators of the white race. Subsequently, they were hated; this is what the narrator simply describes as "[s]weep of human affairs… passed over him and left him broken and helpless as a wreckage disintegrating on a hostile beach," (25). La Guma is referring to apartheid and its racist policies as hostile Sea that fragments anyone that dares to oppose it, and Uncle Doughty becomes one such a casualty. Finally, Police Constable Raalt confronts gender otherness because he does not experience the command that his fellow men have at home. His wife possibly calls the shots at the house. The narrator says Raalt sews his clothes and does the entire house work as the wife looks on (30). The subsequent trauma leads too much to confront without smoking.

The Fragmented self in *A Walk in the Night* also stands out through what Vito Zepenic defines as a "sense of emptiness with a painful intensity in form of flashback." (84). The character harbours no other substance besides painful memories and they cannot be of better use to those around them. This is evident in the character Michael, Willieboy, Joe and Franky Lorenzo.

Michael's self is shattered by anger, self-pity and bitterness as he loiters in Hanover Street on this night. When he meets Uncle Doughty, Michael completely fails to establish a warm conversation. The oldman tries to offer him a drink, but he retorts, "I don't want to drink your wine!" (26). Doughty observes that Michael has a foul mood, which is a reference to his fragmented self. Michael then takes the liquour "with a burst of viciousness" (26) and the narrator adds that "anger mixed with headiness of the liquor" Michael had taken at the pub. He takes an indifferent attitude towards Uncle Dought's earnest and compassionate account of his pathetic situation. For example, after the old man's narration of his glorious past, Michael snarls, "[y]ou old white bastard!" such references to the old man's race gives a hint into the probable cause of Michael's bitterness. There ensues a short jostle over the bottle of wine and blinded by fury, Michael strikes Uncle Doughty (28) and he dies instantly. Moreover, Michael's use of curse words reflects the emptiness of self that Zepenic refers to. After meeting the police, he says mentally, "[t]o hell with him, the lot of them," (43) to express his distaste for the white people.

Willieboy is another self whose emptiness is exhibited by anger, bitterness and melancholy memories through flashbacks. At Miss Gipsy's hotel, he picks a quarrel with the Sailors; his argument is that they are foreigners poised to defile coloured girls (53). He lunges at the Pueto Rican Seaman nearly stabbing him had he not stumbled on the table. As he moves out of the hotel, the narrator clarifies that he has always been aware of his inferiority. He has seen others climb the societal ladder, but "emerged from dreams mingling with the noisy crowd" (73). Willieboy is fragmented by class- the poor of the poorest in District six. When he meets Mr Green, he demands that he gives him money and beats him up (74). It is after the two violent instances that he comes face to face with the white the police officer, Raalt. He is searching for the Uncle Doughty's murderer and using Abraham's hint, he assumes Willieboy is the suspect and shoots him. As he lies in the van bleeding, Willieboy goes into flashbacks. As Zepenic argues, the reader observes painful memories of Willieboy's past. His father used to assault his mother and she did the same to him. One day he had not eaten anything and hawked newspapers. He was given a commission to buy fish. When her mother realized this, she "slapped him again and again," (76). The father was always drunk and after beating the mother, he would beat Willieboy too.

Similarly, Joe is another self whose self is shattered by painful memories. He is the poorest of the novella's characters and to suggest his permanent vagrancy, the narrator describes him as having "soft brown eyes of a dog" (9). Like Willieboy, Joe's self-esteem is shattered by his poverty. He reminds Michael that one does not have to be a thief just because of problems since everyone has "troubles." To sum up his troubles, he says: "I got nothing. No house, no people, no place. Maybe that's trouble. Don't I say?" (69). When Michael still doubts him, he narrates the melancholy history of his life. Joe's father left one morning and did not return. He had no job, but with a family to provide for; they had never paid rent and so the landlord evicted them and their furniture was taken away (72). Michael realizes that as Joe narrates these experiences, he assumes a melancholy expression of face. Finally, Franky Lorenzo is described as a person that is angry with himself; when the wife tells him that he is expectant, he shouts at her (36). They have five children and his wife Grace has just conceived the sixth child. Could his anger have stemmed from the wife's pregnancy?

In Fanon's perspective, these characters' fragmented natures stem from aspects of otherness in their settings. Michael's anger possibly stems from the racial otherness he has experienced at the work place and the system's treatment of Africans in District Six. He wonders why his boss does not expect him to rest (4). When he meets the white police, they demand that he shows them his "dagga" and ruffle him up like a criminal. When they find him with money, they demand to know where he has stolen it. In their opinion, a black person is a thief and drug junkie. Citing Jan Mohamed, Breidlid argues that in racially polarized society, "the individual is treated generically" (111). He implies that racial otherness drives Michael to transfer rage against the white race to the innocent Uncle Doughty. At the surface value Willieboy's bitter experiences with parents suggest that his traumatic experiences emanate from age and class otherness. His mother possibly relegates him because he is a child; however the real cause of his alienation is racial otherness as propagated by apartheid. In the flashback, Willieboy reveals that his father always drank before assaulting the mother. In order to "reconstruct the non- self" typical of the subaltern state (Breidlid, 110), Willieboy's father turns her mother into a punching bag for his aggression against the whites. Joe's situation also stems from race rather than class; his poverty echoes Fanon's words: "in the colonies, the economic substructure is also a superstructure. You are rich because you are white, you a white because you are rich," (40). Fanon therefore suggests that blacks are poor because they are black and are black because they are poor and that is Joe's situation. He represents the poverty ridden black race of South Africans doomed by their race to be indigent. Fanky Lorenzo is neither bitter because of the child nor poverty. The narrator says he "worked like hell in the docks," (37), but earns peanuts because he is coloured.

The Non-self Self and the Mental: the Body as the Other in *A Walk in the Night*

The domineering presence of the self tends to compel marginalized characters to exist mostly at the mental rather than physical realms, which diminishes their ability to exist as normal human persons. In his analysis of Michael Adonis, Bredlib observes:

> When he meets the police, Michael, mentally fights back: 'white son of a bitch. I'll get him.' He avoids direct confrontation with the police since the end result is given. His position as an underdog is clearly and realistically exposed. He defines himself in relation to Raalt and Andries and situates himself within the oppressor oppressed dichotomy [...] he loses his normal urge to resist and slides into 'internal angry monologues. (107)

The racist system cannot condone the existence of a healthy assertive self among the marginalized and any attempt by Michael to physically oppose Raalt will result in his death. He therefore resorts to mental resistance through monologues that bolster his mental activities. After he leaves the police, Michael mentally curses, "you mucking Boer...you mucking bastard boer, with your mucking gun... (12), which demonstrates his hyperactive mind at the expense of his body. There is emphasis on their mental activity instead of physical resistance, which echoes Liang's description of the schizoid as person that has undergone a split between the body and mind and is only capable of mental operations (69). As a result essential relationships such as marriage are relegated because they do not bolster mental activities. This section usurps Liang's employs of the embodied self to analyse psychological consequence of racial otherness on La Guma's characters in *A Walk in the Night*.

Most of the characters in la Guma's novella have given up marriage and focused on what Laing refers to as mental operations or activity. The prime mover, Michael Adonis has never got married, but only thinks about it as a phantasy typical of his hyperactive mind. In the second person, he goes into a monologue, "[y]ou ought to get yourself a goose," (44), and goes into phantasy about the type of woman he expects. It is an idealized version of a woman, too perfect to be found. Michael cannot imagine leaving his cash to woman with weaknesses. The dialogue continues, "[y]ou ought to get married and have a family," (44). It is this utterance that confirms his singleness. The use of second person is similar to illeism, in which characters address themselves in the third person to suggest the presence of other selves in their consciousness. Andrew Melone observes that illeism is a proof of the trinity in the Christian faith (500) because when Yahweh refers to himself as "Yahweh" then it is possible that another person of the trinity is speaking. The use of "you" transforms Michael's supposed internal monologues to dialogues hence a possible victim of dissociation. When he meets a young woman and is unable to establish a rapport with her, he responds to the voice, "[t]o hell with the lot of them," (46). His mind is focused on mental resistance to otherness that he cannot love a woman and have a family.

Willieboy is another of La Guma's characters that is so removed from realities to connect with the opposite sex. As Breidlid argues concerning Michael's powerlessness, Willieboy could not resist the violence meted out on him by the parents except by the mind; subsequently, he slides into the unembodied self to bolster his mental resistance. He demonstrates a hatred for sex in the mask of morality. When he visits Miss Gipsy's hotel, he is more interested in the wine to ignite his hyperactive mind than the beautiful girls at the hotel (50). He pleads with Gipsy and she gives him cheap wine on credit. Nancy observes that he looks cross (51) to suggest his preoccupation with mental activity rather than physical love. But when the sailors show interest in the girls, he starts criticizing the sailors and Gipsy. He argues that the men are foreigners bent on exploiting coloured girls like Nancy (53). In this hotel Willieboy fulfills Laing's assertion that the unembodied self observes, controls and criticizes anything in relation to what the body is experiencing (74). When the Pueto Rican Sea man touches a coloured girl, Willieboy attacks him (54). He is possibly jealous because he is himself incapable of loving a woman; Laing associates the unembodied self with extreme jealousy.

Joe roams the street alone without any attachment to people in his life. The writer does not mention any interests or thoughts related to the opposite sex except the problems he has suffered. In other words, he solely preoccupied with depression rather than the fine things of life embodied in the opposite sex. Although Joe maintains moral principles and even rejects wine, his mind is stuck on the melancholy history of his life. When he meets Michael before he joins gangsters, Joe told him how his father overwhelmed by family responsibilities woke up one morning and disappeared (69). Since he never paid rent, all their household properties were taken by the landlord and the children went about begging. Although he tells Michael that he has no people he can love, his attachment on Michael attests to the low levels of alienation of his self. He tells Michael, "I am your pal. A man has got a right to look after another man," (75). He replies, "Go to hell. Leave me alone." Michael is the real culprit; he is too unembodied to live among normal human society of people like Joe.

Foxy, scarfaced boy and the Sockies they look for are too unembodied to connect with society through love and marriage. They have chosen substance abuse to bolster their mental activity and detach themselves from normal activities in the body. When Michael joins them, they give him a puff of the drug and "he felt the floor move under him," (78). As Breidlid argues, these boy are the other in a system they cannot resist except mentally (75). Although they are sexually mature, they do not have any relationships with opposite sex except rape. Joe reveals that they rape girls and women. He says, "You don't know those boys. They have done bad things. I heard. To girls, also. I heard about Mrs Kannemeyer's daughter. And they use knives, too (75). Rape is a pointer to sex addiction, which is typical of the unembodied self because it is characterized by flare for what Liang refers to as imagos (73). Victims of this self are addicted to pornography to find sexual pleasure in abstract images (mental pleasure) rather than true feelings for human beings.

Uncle Doughty is another unembodied self both through obsession with art and alcoholism. The bitter racial realities around him possibly have him relegated for marrying a coloured wife and the subsequent trauma drives him into acting. The characters he imitates are other abstract selves that enable him resist the overbearing racist regime. Uncle Doughty resembles David, Laing's patient who acts as a woman to dissipate the trauma arising from his overbearing mother (71). His acting is however a kind of mental resistance against otherness and so is Doughty's experience. By playing the part of Hamlet's father's ghost and other characters in his acting career, he is able to launch his attack at the racist regime he hates with a passion. In Michael's presence he confesses that apartheid has reduced him to the current state of hopelessness. He says, "[t]hat is us Michael my boy. Ghosts doomed to walk the night," (27). His marriage life was possibly childless hence his present loneliness. If so then could his bent on the mental have caused the infertility? After his wife's demise, Uncle Doughty gives his life to alcoholism; to possibly heighten his mental hyperactivity and overcome the trauma. The only woman he loves is the memory of his late wife and the plays he performed in Britain, Australia and South Africa.

Conclusion

A Walk in the Night is not just a Marxist interpretation of the South African society under Western imperialism. The constant association of La Guma's works with class struggle and revolution by proletariat is a blindfold that prevents readers from appreciating these works from other perspectives like post-colonial and psychological criticism. It is clear how aspects of otherness, particularly racial otherness, destroy the psyches of characters consigning them to substance abuse, alcoholism, phantasy and singleness against their will. La Guma is not really concerned with relegation of characters by reason of their class but rather the race to which they belong. When Raalt finds Uncle Doughty in District Six, he is profoundly shocked that a white man should be found in ghetto. This implies that it is the colour of the skin that determines the class of a person in this society. Therefore, Joe, Willieboy and Lorenzo are not poor because they are exploited by the rich as is the case in Marx's Germany, but rather they are black and have to be poor. The thought that they have to suffer because of attributes they are ascribed to magnifies their trauma; hence the fragmented self. Aside from this, the overbearing nature of apartheid diminishes the potential to resist physically and the majority of them opt for mental resistance which accentuates their psychological problems. The so called hybrid resistance by postcolonial scholars such as Bredlid is a fragmented self that resists and submits simultaneously. The instability typical of this fragmented resistance is also a psychological anomaly that also stems from otherness.

1.2 The Shattered Self and Wanner's *London, Cape Town, Joburg*

> Wanner's *London, Cape Town, Joburg* is concerned with the grammar of identity and location; the nature of boundaries, both transitive and intransitive; and navigation as a modality of existence in, and defining both the transitive self and the transnational space. (11)
>
> *Stephen Clingman*

Literary critics delimit Wanner's *London, Cape Town and Joburg* to themes characteristic of migration literature such as cultural hybridity, migration, ambivalence and alienation without an attempt to examine the harrowing impact of othering on the migrants psyche. Indeed Clingman in the above quotation focuses on the novel's attributes of migration literature such as identity and transnationalism. This chapter differs from Clingman's study by examining the psychological impact of some strands othering invented by the migration experience. Transnational migrations place the migrant character at the margins of the host nation and unless they have coping strategies, the subsequent trauma results in self-alienation or the fragmented self.

As observed in the foregoing discussion, characters in La Guma's *A Walk in the Night* undergo internal fragmentation as a result of racial othering that the apartheid regime subjects them. Wanner, however, widens the scope of othering to class and cultural differences that affect migrant characters that migrate from Africa to the West. As much as these marginalized characters do not run mad, they experience traumatic experiences that alter their selves a great deal.

Published in 2014, Zukiswa Wanner's *London, Cape Town, Joburg* is a captivating tale of the harrowing consequences of alienation arising from the cultural mix typical of migration in the modern world. Racial and cultural mix is facilitated by both colonialism and characters' migration from London (1994- 1998), Cape Town (1998-2008) and Johannesburg (2008-2011) that constitute the three parts of the novel. Wanner's major objective is to possibly highlight the fragmenting potential of otherness that stem from cultural mixture and globalization. According to Fanon, otherness causes collapse of characters' psyche (182) hence fragmentation. In short, *London, Cape Town and Joburg* is a story of marginalized persons that exist in a binary opposition with dominant groups. The subsequent feeling of otherness results in fragmented states such as depression, cultural confusion and suicide. The major characters that experience otherness and the fragmented self in the novel are Liam, Martin, Germaine, Zuko, Victoria, Sufyan and Priya.

In her critique on Nuruddin Farah's novels, Fatima Moolla writes:

> In order to achieve closure, however, individual freedom must submit to socialization. The individual here submits to a socially constituted morality, but that submission is presented as the outcome of individual desire…infinite self-reflexivity fragments the self. This fragmentation of the self

is ambiguously represented as both pathological and liberatory. (Moolla 253)

The above quote from Moolla's critique of Farah's novels sums up the features of a shattered self. Moolla suggests that for characters to succeed, "achieve closure", the self should submit to direction and association with others and be ready to submit to moral principles. Violation of norms and isolation shatters the self through depression and other "pathological" conditions that render it ineffective. Citing Charles Taylor, Moolla asserts, "[s]elfhood and good…selfhood and morality [are] inextricably intertwined themes" (13). Moolla therefore questions the individualistic model upon which the novel was invented. She suggests that characters in Farah's novels fail for shunning societal interaction and morality hence nurturing an ineffective pathological self. Devoid of coping strategies, characters are depressed, alienated and rendered hopeless by trauma arising from diverse strands of otherness. Moolla's suggestion applies to all major characters in Wanner's *London, Cape Town and Joburg*.

Vito Zepenic defines the shattered self as a "sense of emptiness with a painful intensity in form of flashback." (84). The self harbours no other substance besides painful memories and the individual cannot be of better use to those around them. At severe levels of depression, the character resorts to suicide to destroy the hopeless self. Zepenic's "self-emptiness" is similar to Moolla's "self-reflexivity" where the individual relegates others and turns focus on the self. Obsessed with the self, the character fails to learn that others also suffer and hence the temptation to commit suicide.

As the novel begins, Germaine, the heroine of the novel spends a lot of time away from the husband, crying. She refuses to sleep in her husband's room and opts for her late son's room. Martin says:

> As soon as the last person left, Germaine shed her first tears. Heartbreaking sobs that shook her whole body. I tried to hold her, but she was rigid in my arms. In our sixteen years together, this was the first time she'd shut me out. And she's been doing so ever since. She no longer sleeps in our room but in his. She hold onto clothes he wore the day before he died, refuses to part with them so that I can throw them in the wash. (9)

Germaine's self has been emptied by the traumatic experiences and her ordeal reiterates Zepenic's concept of the shattered self. Zuko's clothes and room embody the flashbacks that have taken her passion for life. These pathological aspects of Germaine appear at the beginning of the novel, which prompts the reader to account for it. Wanner uses a long flashback to explain the cause of Germaine's fragmented condition. It is amazing to observe that strands of otherness contribute greatly to Germaine's shattered self.

As soon as they arrive in South Africa, Martin, Germaine's husband starts relegating Germaine and his mother's company for his elder brother, Liam and biological father, Mtshali. Martin and Liam believe that identity and paternity issues are patriarchal and therefore women (his mother and wife) should be relegated. Liam tells Martin:

> My father was a great father to both of us but he wasn't your biological father. We're black people even though you think you aren't as black as you look. As black people, there are certain things we need to acknowledge in our culture. We can't ignore our ancestors [...] I am not saying you should be bosom buddies. But I suspect if he dies tomorrow, you'll regret not having reached out. You have sisters you should know. The Lil Cadre in your house has cousins he should get to know. (276)

Liam in this instance gives advice contrary to their mother's perspective. Whereas the mother describes Martin's biological father as callous and abusive (275), Liam underscores the need to reconnect with one's fathers as a pertinent aspect of African culture. The patrilineal attribute of most African culture, for Liam is a formidable foundation upon which every man, martin included, should lean on. The Lil Cadre in the passage is Martin's son, Zuko, who in spite of his biracial identity, has to be introduced to true Mtshalis to get the blessings of African ancestors. Martin therefore relegates his wife and mother and takes his son away to reconnect with his patriarchal ancestry. As he moves away from the mother, he says, "[b]ut sometimes a man has to act and discount the opinions of others" (277). The "others" in this context are the "gender others"- his wife and mother, he has resolved to shove away from his search for patriarchal identity.

Germaine realizes this gender othering and observes, "Martin was getting sentimental about his biological father and against mine and his mother's opinion," (280). He takes their son Zuko to "know his grandpa," (280). The adoptive father that brought him up no longer counts in the patriarchal matrix because it is a woman that chose him. In her mother's perspective, Martin's biological father is devoid of conscience and his sudden interest in Martin has strings attached (280). It does not last long before martin's biological father, Mtshali come up with the idea of Goldtreet, a company that is selling shares. Liam insists that they should use Germaine's company shares, which Martin dismisses and opts to use family savings. When he consults his wife, Germaine, she rejects it out rightly. Martin appeals to patriarchal tradition to otherize the wife. He says, "I decide to bring it up casually after the news one evening. If she says no, I will have to put my foot down as a man and help her realize that it is not about her," (290). Germaine give in and Martin with fellow men continue with their meetings and investments. Martin's biological father then dies and when Martin reads *Mail & Guardian* newspaper and discovers that Goldstreet was a scum. He asserts, "I read all this while sitting in the car and I start sweating. Oh fucking bloody stupid hell. I am one of the fools who has lost all his family's savings on Goldstreet," (313). Liam calls to confirm the same and the only thing he can tell Martin is "Fuuck! That stupid, idiotic old man fooled us," (314). When Germaine gets the news that Martin has lost all family savings, it marks the onset of her pathological condition. She breaks down saying, "I warned you about that bastard," (322). She yells and wants to know whether the rituals that Mtshali had arranged to place charms on martin's waist would bring back their family savings. Gender othering accounts for impoverishment of the family, which Germaine confirms:

> This is another way men abuse women, I kept thinking. This fool that I married had just financially abused me. Everything we had saved, my security, my son's. Everything except the roof over our heads, the measly savings since last year when he did the transaction and his next pay cheque. (324)

This passage makes a direct reference to gender politics as the major cause of Germaine's shattered self. The belief that the man as the head of the house has an upper hand in decision making in the family predisposes many African families to financial mismanagement and subsequent misery. It is odd how Martin "puts down his foot as a man" only to lead Germaine and Zuko to abject poverty. Germaine avoids Martins' company and gets engrossed into her ceramic project. When Martin enquires about her whereabouts, Zuko reports that "she is busy making vaginas" (321). Few days later, another man, Martins elder brother deals a final blow to Martin's hopes in life. His only child, and heir commits suicide and leaves the following note about Liam:

> I loved him as much as I loved my own father and mother. He was the person I ran to when I was angry with my mum for yelling at my dad [...] and then on Saturday it happened [...]. He got in bed with me. I tried to move away, but he pinned me down [...]. Then he pushed my bum open and put his dick in me. I have never felt such pain. (332)

The other man Martin trusts at the expense of his wife and mother defiles his only child; he is unable to tell Martin because the man is Martin's best friend and a powerful politician. Moreover, Germaine is devastated by the fact that Zuko would not open up to her possibly because he had joined the male fraternity and believed in their supremacy. She observes that even the last letter he left was addressed to his father (2). She says, "[n]o reference to me in the address and yet I loved him," (3). She wonders of what benefit Zuko and Martin nurtured the patriarchal bond to relegate persons that may have protected them from peril.

It is this gender othering that drives Germaine to her shattered self that runs through the story. His self is prevailed by hate and painful memories that are severely disabling. Martin observes that she was filled with 'hatred in her eyes and when she "blinks... all I see is pain" (11). She avoids Martin and he misses her a lot, but she no longer cares about the intimacy they have had more than a decade in marriage.

Liam is another character with a pathological self that is fragmented by strands of otherness. A black man born and raised in Britain comes in conflict with racial othering, which leaves him psychological fragmented. At teenage, Liam realizes Martin's naivety and contends that "some people who are not clever may not be nice to others who looked different from them," (140). He has learnt the stigmatization of racial difference in the British populace and the want of coping strategies marks the onset of a pathological self. As Martin strives to acquire fluency in English and French, Liam "took to languages like a duck to water. By the time he was twelve...he could speak to the South Africans we encountered in isiXhosa or Afrikaans," (140). Although at the face value Liam stands out as patriotic, a critical examination of this act is a pathological mechanism adopted to combat racial otherness. This is corroborated by Martins assertion that Liam "got into numerous fights at school," (140) to possibly stop contemporaries that otherized him. His pathological self is further elaborated by Martin's observation that British teachers described him as "aggressive and angry perhaps something many parents of young black men in Western world are familiar with in school reports," (140). The aggression and anger in Liam embodies the alienation that gnaws at Liam's self as a result of racial othering prevalent in the Britain. Apparently, Liam is not the sole victim; most young blacks in their formative years have come to this realization and their selves have started the disintegration process.

Liam's marriage however demonstrates the ambivalence typical of alienated selves. One would expect him to marry an African woman given his spite for the white race; however, he falls in love with a Boer woman and replaced his father's name with his mother's. He became Swart Mokoena, the first being Afrikaan's word for "black" and the surname, his mother's. in his conversation with Germaine, she notes: "[a]nd it was a sordid tale of a gold-digging woman who married a man, had children with him, and then afterwards tried to get him arrested on trumped-up charges because she'd found another lover-an older richer man," (155). His white wife, Jenny, jilts him for an older richer lover, which prompt him to swear that he will never marry again. Class othering therefore plays an essential role in accentuating Liam's pathological self. Germain asserts that he is very bitter and rants about racial segregation even where other strands of othering manifest (158). Liam holds pathological relationships with the opposite sex and is a possible cause of his propensity to defile Zuko and the so called adopted son, Mxolisi. The narrator describes him as having the "sweetest, saddest face," (124). This sulky facial expression symbolizes Mxolisi's self-fragmentation arising from age and class otherinng. Liam takes advantage of his class and age to defile him. He is the house keeper's son; the father cannot afford to pay his fees and so falls prey to the Liam's predatory instincts.

Martin is another casualty of othering conditions that fragment his self. Born in Ireland and raised by an Irish adoptive father, Martin comes face to face with othering conditions of racial and cultural mould that alter his self. As he grows up in Richmond, London, it dawns on Martin that his adoptive father's class cannot shield him from the racially polarized cultural conditions. He says:

> One day, I must've been about four or five, I was walking in Hyde Park with my dad. And some stranger who was walking with his friend looked at me, looked at my dad and said out loud, 'Bloody hell, that's a really black child…ow, would you look at that, mate? An Irish man and his little monkey.' My father lunged at him, but as though by some miracle, a policeman appeared out of nowhere and eventually clamed everyone down. But then I was crying. (139)

In this episode, Zukiswa captures what Staszak describes as stigmatization of basic differences into othering. Martin's racial differences are stigmatized by the white stranger into an other. The stranger perceives Martin as too black to fit in the Irish populace and assigns him the role of the other. He started learning that there were the self- the Irish- and the Other, the blacks (140). Martin's breakdown reiterates Fanon's assertion on the alteration of the psyche by othering conditions (182). Martin's self-fragmentation begins this day and he wants to protect his son Zuko from a similar ordeal. He says, "I wanted to protect him from the worst that the world had to offer," (142). It is evident that Martin's self has never recovered from the childhood ordeal that reserved for him the role of the other. In other words, he is destitute of requisite coping strategies to coexist with the dominant group. For Moolla, the want of coping strategies results in self-reflexivity, which is pathological (253). Martin lives in constant fear that his son may be attacked because of his biracial identity. He says:

> I love London. But I had heard one too many stories of teenage boys and girls and boys attacking people at train stations. I did not want him to grow up to be one of them, or equally worrisome-be the one attacked. I figured the best thing to do was to take him to a place where there were more people who looked like him, and where I had the support structure of an extended family. I discuss it with Germaine and, being an adventurous spirit, she is game. (142)

Racial othering compels Martin to embrace the belief that London is not home. It is a psychological anomaly, a kind of phobia out of the childhood ordeal. It triggers Martin's desire to migrate back to Africa in search for his original identity. Migration literature scholars such as William Safran assert that immigrants such as Martin can only find peace through return migrations to their homelands (83-84). This is illustrated in Martin's claim that his son can only mature well where "more people look like him" and "there is support structure of the extended family." Such decisions can only be sound in absence of pathological symptoms such as phobia as is the case in Martin. He makes a fateful decision basing on a psychological condition that plunges the family in fiasco.

Stuart Hall contends that the return to Africa is neither haven of peace nor panacea to restoration of one's identity. He writes, "[c]ultural identity is not a fixed essence at all lying unchanged outside history and culture... it is not once-and for-all. It is not a fixed origin on which we can make some final and absolute Return," (395).

Indeed when Martin returns to South Africa, racial othering is worse than in England. Martin says, "[i]t is madness to discover that the one place where I have been made to feel my race the most is the place where the majority of the population looks like me," (180). Whereas Directors like Graham are qualified for their jobs, Manager Jaco in South Africa "hasn't finished high school" (181) but had a vocational training unrelated to banking. When he starts his marketing job of bringing to the bank wealthy clients, all of them are rejected until he unearths the cause of his plight through Michelle: racism. All the managers that rejected Martin's clients including Mr Oothuizen retract their earlier decisions when Michelle asks them to account for their action (182). Over lunch, she recounts her experience of how she was made to "run around doing almost nothing" (182) until in a party she came along with her black husband. One of the directors asked, "Mrs Michaels, is that your husband? ...forgive me, we thought you were colored," (183).

She was promoted and handed greater responsibilities after they knew that she was not mixed race. Black people are favored in South Africa and biracial people are relegated.

Socially, Zuko is not happy with life in the so called mother nation. In his personal journal, he says that the decision to migrate to South Africa separates him from his friends in England (240). He also reveals that he is haunted by images of violence he has seen on television in South Africa. He sees the graphic image of a man being lynched during the xenophobic attacks in the country (239). It is in this very mother nation that Martin confronts the saddest moments of his life. It is while in his supposed paradise- the ancestral land that he says, "[a] part of me has been ripped apart, stepped on, thrown into the rubbish bin. And just when I think I am almost fine...my son and heir is dead and it is all my fault," (6). Zuko commits suicide and Martin descends to the lowest stave of his family life. He is guilty and as much as he probably singles out negligence as his mishap, the return to the ancestral land is the true culprit. Clingman aptly observes that Martin "navigates the space between the roots of his family and homeland and his European cultural home and finds belonging in neither space" (224). He is unhappy in England and South Africa and therefore occupies Homi Bhabha's liminal space. Before taking his life, Zuko reveals that he has been sexually abused by Martin's elder brother, Liam. Migration to South Africa brings the family to sex pests.

1.3 Suicide and the Fragmented Self and Farah's *Close Sesame*

It is quite conventional to define suicide as the murder of oneself possibly because of a dislike of one's living conditions or rejection by a loved one. The individual decides to end their lives because of the subsequent despair they confront after the cessation of a moment of happiness. Emerging psychological conversations nonetheless view suicide as destruction of a despicable or indispensable self within. The primary self finds it impossible to exist with the other self and resorts to murder to eradicate it. This chapter extends the conversation that suicide is a consequence of internal conflicts in which characters strive to annihilate the "other" self within. Using psychological criticism, the chapter provides new evidence from Nuruddin Farah's *Close Sesame*. The ideas of Jacques Lacan and Karl Menninger will form theoretical basis of interpretation. The major finding of the chapter is that suicide is not spite for oneself, but for the other despicable or beloved self coexisting with the primary self that can only be eradicated through death.

Suicidal episodes such as Zuko's in *London, Cape Town and Joburg* as presented in the previous chapter will mostly be interpreted as Zuko's decision to kill himself. This chapter contends that Zuko does not kill the primary self, but the 'other self' nurtured by his cultural surroundings that he hates. Zuko's ordeal resembles Mitsusaburo's friend in Kenzaburo Oe's *Silent Cry* and Florence's mother in Safi Abdi's *A Mighty Collision of Two Worlds*. Oe notes that Mitsusaburo's friend in *Silent Cry* "could not reconcile himself with his inner turmoil, painted his head crimson" and placing a cucumber in his anal region, hanged himself (18). The context of the story reveals that he had migrated from Japan to pursue further studies at Columbia University where he started experiencing psychological anomalies. At the mental asylum, the nurse constantly assaults all the patients. Florence's mother loved her father so much that when he leaves with another woman, she commits suicide. Anisa, wonders why a woman should kill herself just because a man has left her (44). Anisa does not think about the other woman with whom Florence's father flirted and abandoned the mother. Similarly, the character Othello in Shakespeare's *Othello* takes the sword and commits suicide when he realizes that the white man, Iago has tricked him to kill his innocent wife Desdemona. At the face value, these characters kill themselves, but psychological scholars dispute this conversation.

According to Karl Menninger, suicide is an attempt to kill the significant other, that is the love or despicable object they have incorporated in the making of the self (Cited from Davison, 252). The patient's self- esteem subsides to the state of a deserted infant that yearns to "annihilate the incorporated love object" (252). In Menninger's view, Fresha has Frank's self as the significant other that she has incorporated in the formation of the self and she finds it difficult to live without this other self after the break up. The suicide is not killing herself, but a futile attempt to eradicate this other self (Frank) that has become inseparable. This is the case in Florence's mother's experience.

Jacques Lacan incorporates the role of the Other in alienation of the self. He uses the analogy of the infant that starts as something inseparable from its mother because it has no sense of self or individualized identity (Cited from Rafey Habib, 7). When the baby looks at the mirror, it is able to recognize its image. It sees it as the ideal image; a complete form of the object (baby) and conceptualizes it as the other. The baby is now capable of distinguishing the *I* from the *other*, which is estrangement from oneself and the mother who is the Other. Anika Lenaire expounds that the moment of identification is to Lacan a moment of jubilation because the baby has the ideal image of itself, but is also accompanied by a depressive reaction when the infant contrast its helpless state to the omnipotence of the mother. The infant learns that there is an outside something...an Other on whom it is dependent. The awareness of separation or the fact of otherness creates an anxiety; a sense of loss- an alienation. The baby's attempt to revert to the original sense of fullness with the mother is impossible because it is now consciously aware that an Other exists (161-167). This sense of otherness is the condition for the baby to emerge as an independent subject or self.

According to Lacan, the mother plays an essential role in the alienation of the infant and therefore Angelika and the other woman contribute greatly to Florence mother's suicide. Their presence brings a mirror to the fore through which Florence's mother see their weaknesses, which inscribes "the other" in their consciousness. The other woman sets off the formation of the "ugly other" in Florence's mother's consciousness. Similarly, the realisation that Iago has tricked Othello to kill his innocent wife sets off the emergence of the "gullible other" in Othello's consciousness, which he hates. He does not therefore kill himself, but the despicable "other" within.

Yiannis Gabriel asserts that the Lacanian theory introduces Self- othering because the child sees its image as the other just as the unconscious is the stranger within ourselves (Para 6). When people confront otherness and the trauma thereof, they encounter self othering which may result in the fragmented self. Gabriel adds that that "[s]ometimes a man has no choice but silence or even kill the woman in him." In other words, the awareness of Otherness by marginal groups creates an anxiety, a sense of loss and hence suicide. This is a possible cause of psychological conflicts that result in suicide in Mitsaburo's friend in *Silent Cry*. He is probably marginalized by host communities when he migrates from Japan. This subchapter extends the conversation that suicide is a consequence of internal conflicts in which characters strive to annihilate the "other" self within. Using psychological criticism, the article provides new evidence from Buchi Emecheta's *The Joys of Motherhood*, Nuruddin Farah's *Close Sesame*, Brian Chikwava's *Harare North*. The ideas of Jacques Lacan and Karl Menninger will form theoretical basis of interpretation. The study is a library research that proceeds through close reading of the three primary texts, secondary texts and refereed journals. The major finding of the study is that suicide is not spite for oneself, but for the other despicable or beloved self coexisting with the primary self that can only be eradicated through death.

Annihilation of the other Self: Suicide and the Detestable "other" in Self

Selves that feel different in relation to others may end up isolating themselves even without anyone discriminating against them. The feeling of otherness is inscribed within the self in relation to the Other around them. A man who is infertile will compare his self to fertile men and noticing the difference, isolates himself even without being discriminated against. Mary Canales defines this as self othering, which is accurate because the barren women in her study contrast their selves with the fertile Others that unconsciously show them the mirror that compel them to see their barren selves. The result is magnification of a "barren other" in their consciousness, which their true self detests. The internal conflict is between "the self" and "the barren other" that is magnified by "the fertile Other" in the community. Tara Couineau and Alice Domar submit that personal difference (infertility) and social pressures combine to create emotional turmoil that come with harmful social and psychological consequences (296). The victims may isolate themselves from society and the feelings of helplessness and depression may follow.

Demolition of Love Object: Suicide and Intimate "other" in Self

This subsection takes Menninger's trajectory that views suicide as an attempt to eradicate the love object the person has incorporated in the formation of the self with reference to Chikwava's *Harare North* and Farah's *Close Sesame*.

Deeriye, the hero of Farah's *Close Sesame* has had bitter experiences in life and after the demise of his wife; there are people he loves with great passion. His son Mursal and daughter, Zeinab are so much part of him that he cannot live without them. When he gets worried of Mursal's death, he is so affected that he gets in hypnotic trance:

> Yaziid; Mucaawiya; the constitution of the city of Medina; Mina and the act of stoning; the minaret which was concrete: stone; Satan's *rajüm;* the blessing of the martyred ones beginning in this case with Mukhtaar and Jibril Mohamed- Somali; and finally Mursal: all carriers of the message, the irony being they didn't see themselves as conveyers of the Message of the Living One. (222)

In the trance he feels that he should be happy for his dearest friends that have died in the fight against the wicked, dictatorial regime. He is persuaded that in spite of his love, he should see them as martyrs: Mukhtaar, who goes against his clan and father to oppose the dictator; Jibril, a former army officer who is shot while planting a bomb adjacent to the president's residence, Mursal, his son; the undisputable leader of the underground movement that vows to use violence against the regime and disappears mysteriously. The trance suggests that they have died for a cause and have a reward in paradise. This implies that those who cower (like Deeriye) and continue to compromise with the evil political system may never see paradise. Earlier on, the self of his late wife Nadiifa tells him to finish the job, which his son had failed. She suggests that Mursal is another self within Deeriye: "the duelists are your two selves" (249), which are Mursal's and Deeriye's primary self. Deeriye confesses to Zeinab, his daughter:

> I am a collage of many notions and some are yours and some of them are Mursal's and some Nadiifas's and some come from Natasha and some from Rooble; and so someone never goes away forever- one can always call that part of oneself, which is from the vanished person and talk to *it* or *him* or *her.* We are

not only ourselves, we are *others* too, those whom we love, those have influenced our lives, who have made us what we are. (253-254)

This passage suggests that excessive love for others paves way for their incorporation in the formation of a new self. Deeriyes love for his children and friends has possibly fragmented him such that he cannot live without them. The italicization of *it, him, her* and *others* is a possible reference to "other selves" that coexist with his primary host. Although Nadiifa passed on, he has always inquired of her to advise him. As Nadiifa reveals, Mursal is now in conflict with his self and she says "[y]ou are not sure of anything anymore," (249).

When Mursal disappears, Deeriye sinks in a chronic depression that is followed by a hallucinatory experience. He cannot sleep the whole night (247), but when they switch off the light, Nadiifa speaks to him. Deeriye portrays his fragmentation when he just rises up the following morning and decides to go and make an attempt at the General's life. Throughout the story, he has consistently spoken against the use of violence, but now he picks Mohamed Somali's revolver to go and kill. Critics have interpreted Deeriye's decision at this moment as suicide contrary to the perspectives that appraise his courage and determination to liberate his community. Derek Wright observes that "Deeriye's death is ambiguous in its significance," as it is not clear whether it is "suicide or failed assassination" (189). However, going by the antecedents to the ordeal for example, death of Mukhtaar, detention of his best friend, Rooble and now the death of his only son Mursal, it is not unreasonable to conclude that his death is suicide. As aforementioned, he cannot live without Mursal, Nadiifa, Rooble, Mohamed Somali, Mukhtaar and other like-minded selves that he has incorporated in his consciousness. Perhaps in death will he usurp his self from their intimacy. Although he had earlier criticized Mahad for solely attempting to shoot the president, Deeriye repeats the same *kamikaze* antic and the General's bodyguards "empty cartridges of machine gun fire on him until the body is nearly cut in half" (260).

Deeriye's ordeal stems from ethnic and political victimization that traverses from the colonial to post independence regimes. His clan opposed Italian invasion and suffered under colonial rule. When the General takes over, he perpetuates colonial policy of divide and rule by favouring collaborators of the colonial regime and relegating those who resisted like Deeriye, Mohamed Somali, Mukhtaar, and his son Mursal. The relegation is evident in the arrest and murder of Mursal, which is unbearable to Deeriye. His depressive episodes only become severe and palpable whenever the authorities adversely affect a member of his underground movement, which implies that Deeriye would be free from depression if the authorities ruled fairly and justly

Annihilation of the other Self: Suicide and the Detestable "other" in Self

Selves that feel different in relation to others may end up isolating themselves even without anyone discriminating against them. The feeling of otherness is inscribed within the self in relation to the Other around them. A man who is infertile will compare his self to fertile men and noticing the difference isolate himself even without being discriminated against. Mary Canales defines this as self othering, which is accurate because the barren women in her study contrast their selves with the fertile Others that unconsciously show them the mirror that compel them see their barren selves. The result is magnification of a "barren other" in their consciousness, which their true self detests. The internal conflict is between "the self" and "the barren other" that is magnified by "the fertile Other" in the community. Tara Couineau and Alice Domar submit that personal difference (infertility) and social pressures combine to create emotional turmoil that come with harmful social and psychological consequences (296). The victims may isolate themselves from society and the feelings of helplessness and depression may follow

In Farah's *Close Sesame*, Deeriye undergoes self othering when he comes in conflict with a superior military power from the white race. Unaware and unprepared for a militarily superior enemy, the young sultan is shocked by the racial arrogance and crude military methods the Italians employ to subjugate his people. As soon as he refuses to release the young man who had killed an Italian soldier, the Italian administrator storms out of the home and an evening later there is a pandemonium, shouts and boom of bazookas (41). The activities in the fore mentioned episode in Lacan's perspective raise a mirror for Deeriye to behold his "other" self. Like the mother in Lacan's analogy, Italians show Deeriye that they are omnipotent and he is a weak, black leader. The dictatorial and cruel experiences prove his weakness and his unconscious inscribes the inferior, African "other" that sets off an internal conflict.

The presence of a superior military European power magnifies the anxiety as he contrasts their powerfulness with his powerlessness and Deeriye isolates himself (self othering) in prayer (41). The narrator says, "[h]e went down on his knees, and he prayed and prayed and prayed. He was alone," (41). Self otherness drives Deeriye to religious fanaticism. His psychic defenses collapse and he starts hearing voices while praying (41-42). Deeriye descends in constant depressions and hallucinatory experiences.

The depression also manifests through the suicide motif, which Deeriye and fellow revolutionaries opt for as a strategy of resistance. Although oppressed characters deliberately choose it as strategy to change their political future, the desire to risk one's life for a course in *Close Sesame* arises from the fragmented self. After getting the news of Mahad's failed assassination attempt, he complains constantly about everything. His self is hopeless about the failure; had it succeeded, Deeriye would have celebrated. When his daughter Zeinab wants him to go for a walk at Bar Novecento, he works himself into an asthmatic fit (96). Later, the narrator reveals that Deeriye hates the rumour that Mukhtaar has betrayed the dissident movement. When Mursal disappears, Deeriye sinks in a chronic depression that is followed by a hallucinatory experience. He cannot sleep the whole night (247), but when they switch off the light, Nadiifa's comes to him. Deeriye portrays his fragmentation when he just rises up the following morning and decides to go and make an attempt at the General's life. Throughout the story, he has consistently spoken against the use of violence, but now he picks Mohamed Somali's revolver to go and kill. Although he had earlier criticized Mahad, Deeriye repeats the same *kamikaze* attempt and the General's bodyguards "empty cartridges of machine gun fire on him until the body is nearly cut in half" (260). Like other revolutionaries, Deeriye hates the "feeble and cowardly other" within that the highhanded colonial and the General regimes have nurtured in him. His religious self and Nadiifa condemn cowardice and praise Mursal and Mohamed Somali and heroes that have confronted evil to their graves.

Mahad is another revolutionary that finds it unbearable for his family to suffer under Italian oppression and the General's oppression consecutively. It hurts him to know that his father died for a course that has never been attained. His father wrestled an Italian soldier who tried to force his way into a Sultan's house and a stray bullet releeased during the scuffle killed the Italian soldier. The father was detained and killed by the colonial government and so Mahad seems to harbor revulsion against the colonial and General's regime for their consistency in creating a "cowardly or inferior other" in his consciousness. It is not surprising that he wants to effect an assassination without any prior planning. Mursal says that Mahad has just listened to the General's speech when in an unpremeditated act of madness grabs the revolver from the General's bodyguard and tries to shoot the General (83). Deeriye refers to Mahad's action a *kamikaze* attack, which is an allusion to suicide missions that were sent by the Japanese soldiers to destroy Allied ships at sea towards the end of the Second World War. In Lacan's perspective, suicide bomber missions arise from a desire to destroy the "feeble and inferior other" that has been natured by the overbearing superiors (Other) around. The presence of highhanded colonial and General's regimes nurtures the "inferior other" in Mahad, which constantly alienates him such that he feels it can only be eradicated by suicide.

Jibril Mohamed Somali possibly belongs to Deeriye's clan, which has been relegated both in the colonial days and General's regime. Felix Mnthali observes that "the General uses tactics of divide and rule through both cooption and ethnic rivalries," (60). Mohamed Somali's clan is therefore relegated such that he has witnessed the suffering of his people for a long time. Frustrated, he spends most of his time and money drinking. The regime trains Somali, like Deeriye and Mahad to always fear the ruling clan. He tries to plant a "time-bomb" near the General's residence, but when he is found and ordered to raise his hands, he attempts to pick his revolver and is shot, but does not die until he shoots one of the soldiers from the ground (218-219). Somali's decision to single handily attempt the General's life arises from spite for the "cowardly other" within that the autocratic regime has nurtured for decades.

Finally, Mursal's decision to endorse the use of violence against the General's regime is suicidal rather than heroic in *Close Sesame*. Deeriye disapproves of Mursal's decision to use force against the regime possibly because he knows the underground movement lacks the resources and organization to fight the regime. When Rooble tells Deeriye of Mursal's intention to use force, he replies, "[t]hey are up to no good," (48). In an argument with Mursal,

Deeriye insists that rather than use force, he is ready to negotiate with the General for Rooble's release. Mursal sees this as the cowardice typical of many members of his clan and even reminds Deeriye how he often said he would not negotiate with the tyrant (194). Mursal defies his father and works with fellow radical members like Mohamed Somali to show spite for the "cowardly other" in their consciousness. When Mohamed is killed, a letter is found on his corpse addressed to Mursal (219). The regime uses this as justification to arrest and kill Mursal. In a hallucination, Deeriye justifies Mursal's death as triumph over the cowardly other. In the hallucination, Somali, Mukhtaar and Mursal are possibly compared to heroes that stone Satan at Mecca (256). They overcame "the cowardly other" to confront the regime and although they did not overthrow it, they free their selves from the despicable other. They are proclaimed saints, far better than Deeriye that still entertains it.

Conclusion

Suicide is not therefore the desire to kill the primary self, but rather another self alongside the host self that gains entrance after a mirthful or melancholic experience that affects the character's psyche. Whereas love is a positive experience, it probably affects the psyche such that the persons one loves so dearly enter and coexist with the primary self. Frank's self therefore bonds so strongly with Fresha's that death is the only available option if she is to get rid of it. Deeriye has so much loved his son Mursal that death is the sole means of ridding off Mursal. In the same way, the presence of dominant groups act as mirrors that create despicable others in the marginalized's consciousness, which may only be eradicated by suicide. Mitsusaburo and Nnu Ego so hate the "inferior other" and "barren other" respectively that only death may eradicate them from their consciousness.

Chapter Two

Fragmented Natures in Selected works of African Drama

Introduction
In the previous chapter, focus on the nexus between otherness and the fragmented self has been on selected works of prose fiction. This chapter will focus on the nexus between strands of othering and the fragmented selves on selected works of drama. The consistent analysis of prose works gives the impression that African playwrights have not explored the nexus between strands of othering and the mental health of characters. African playwrights have delved into this thesis to demonstrate Fanon's argument that the cultural context severely affects the self of characters. These playwrights support Donald Robert's observation that the tendency to locate the source of madness within the patient deflects critical insight away from the culture (iii). Other than personal weaknesses, the political and social setting has a great impact on the characters' psyche. This chapter's focus is how the cultural context affects the selves of characters in John Ruganda's *Shreds of Tenderness* and David Mulwa's *Inheritance*.

Othering and the Fragmented Self in John Ruganda's *Shreds of Tenderness*

Set in an African nation after independence, *Shreds of Tenderness* is a heartrending tale of the effects of political upheavals on the psyche of the marginal groups. A dictator overthrows the government and introduces an autocratic regime that is repressive and intolerant to divergent political ideology. He introduces a totalitarian regime that silences all who want democracy through a strong spying network. Using the older son in the Witu family, the tyrant detains the father, assassinates him. Using his henchman, Mohamed Ali, he trails Wak, Witu's next of kin who goes to exile. Mohamed Ali, turns on Odie, has him arrested and tortured for being Wak's brother. Debilitated by the instruments of torture and a six month detention, Odie looks on as Ali flirts with his only sister, Stella. One thing that disheartens Odie is that his ploy to revenge against Witu and Wak for relegating him for his academic weaknesses is utter fiasco. Indeed Wak suffers in exile as refugees are only defined by the foreign state as aliens and abjects. They are the political others without basic rights of citizens. As much as Odie upholds the notion that citizens who remain in nations under political animosity are more subjected to psychological trauma, Wak underscores that exiles' experiences are worse and more traumatic as a result of the alienation typical of diasporic experience. Wak is compelled to join the revolutionary movement and through a series of sporadic attacks overthrow the dictator and return home. Odie's psychological instability is accentuated not just by the tyrants' detention and torture, but age othering in childhood and the guilt of coming face to face with Wak the democrat. With the victory of the revolutionaries, stayees that compromise the dictator's excesses become the other, which comes with psychological consequences. The play ends when Odie descends into hallucinatory confessions of having betrayed Wak and his father to wreak a revenge because the father loved Wak and otherized him.

Otherness and the Fragmented characters in *Shreds of Tenderness*

In the play *Shreds of Tenderness* Ruganda raises the curtain over the impact of diverse strands of othering and how they pulverise the selves of characters. It is evident that fragmentations of selves from mild strains such as depression to severe ones like hallucinatory experiences arise from relegation of groups and individuals to the marginal spaces. Ruganda singles out age and political othering and demonstrates their psychological impact on characters.

Age othering is the relegation of a group or individual because of his age. Kim Snow asserts that children are oppressed because their situation meets the criteria of the oppressed group: structural oppression (exploitation, marginalization, powerlessness; systematic oppression), cultural imperialism and violence (96). Odie's father, Witu detests Odie because of his weak intellectual ability and continuously stigmatizes him at a young age. The cultural landscape in which Witu hails apparently views adults as embodiments of perfection and the child as the imperfect specimen to be forced to be improved through ridicule and abuse. When Odie does not perform well in class, Witu degrades him in expletives and praises Wak. In a hallucinatory experience, Odie reveals why he revenges against Wak:

> You are a perfect replica of your mother's IQ. Can't think beyond broken breaths in the dark. Look here, young man, I can teach monkeys modern mathematics but you prefer the hind quarters of some… thirty seven out of forty. Remarkable achievement, young man. (*addresses the mangled frame of his father's picture*). I'll try harder, papa. I promise, I'll

> try harder, Papa, only give me a chance. Mother's IQ, ticks
> and termites… (Continues in mime). (129)

In this episode, Wak demands to know why, his brother Odie decides to betray him to the State Research Bureau, the tyrants' secret agents. Odie descends into a hallucination to reveal the traumatizing ordeal of his childhood. Whereas as Wak was academically brilliant, Odie was weak and the father puts blame on his late mother. Witu absolves himself from blame, bragging of his exceptional aptitude that can teach monkeys mathematics as Odie tails in class for inheriting his daft mother. Odie becomes the other in the family because of demonstrating weak academic ability in class. His pleas for the father's understanding fall on deaf ears and he remains an object of derision and contempt. In the family, he is regarded as a failure. He tells Stella, "[t]he old man loved you very much Stella. He really did, you and your stepbrother. In fact, very proud of the two of you. With me it was different. Regarded me a failure. An embarrassment to the family," (30). Witu takes advantage of his age to create a binary situation in the family. Those children who are brilliant in school such as Stella and Wak are favoured: the one that is weak in class is assigned the role of the other and denied certain privileges. When Wak wants to know why Odie betrayed the Father, he says:

> The man never loved me that is why. He always thought I was a disgrace to the family, a big embarrassment. You know it. Everybody knew it. he never bothered to find out why I wasn't doing well at the university. Our strike was the last straw. Good excuse for him to wash his hands off me. He would have found a scholarship for me if he had wanted, couldn't he? But what did he do? Nothing. Absolutely nothing despite mum's entreaties. (120)

Among the Witus, there are children that are given preferential treatment and have rights to all rights and privileges and those relegated to the marginal space. Odie belongs to the latter space and for Fanon, such persons are denied humanity and it is incumbent upon them to resist the oppression or risk psychic collapse (250). At elementary school, the father accuses him of being as daft as the mother and this could be the root cause of his angry and restive nature at university. Indeed Odie does not take it lying down; he takes advantage of the political turmoil to fight back. Being the other, Odie does not deserve to be next of kin in spite of being the first son. Witu abuses his powers as an adult to violate the culture of the community by handing all the inheritance to Wak. Stella says:

> As the next of kin, Odie. As the next male relative, you stood to benefit. Dad is dead, so is Wak. And a younger sister who is not twenty-one yet. And you know Wak was the heir of Dad's estates, though he was six years younger. There was a bit of fracas about it, I remember. But dad, did it in good faith, not because he loved you less. So armed with the photograph and the radio announcement which was also published in the dailies, you confront the officials at the Lands and Survey office to change the land title deed. (20-21)

It will be unreasonable to adopt Stella's attitude without a critical look at Witu's decision to relegate and hold Odie in contempt. As aforementioned, Odie is the other just because he is not as academically brilliant as Wak, which is inconsistent to African philosophy of placing value to humanity. The moral rather than academic ability forms the basis of determining human value in most African communities. Being the first wife's son and weak in academics cannot justify the constant relegation and devaluation from as next of kin. In this frank discussion with Stella, Odie reminds her that her academic ability notwithstanding, she is destitute of the moral foundation to perpetuate her father's repute. He singles out Stella's affair with Mohamed Ali, the soldier who signed their father's death warrant. Odie at this point reiterates the African criteria of using the moral campus to determine merit. In other words, he suggests that his father's criterion of determining the next-of kin was misguided by Western maxims. As much as it is absurd to usurp age othering to justify Odie's crimes such as informing on Wak and his father Witu, it is equally imprudent to single out Odie's weaknesses without referring to it. It is conventional for scholars to squarely blame Odie's criminal record and pathological tendencies on personal crevices without any consideration of the othering in his immediate family.

As a result of age-othering Odie is not just depressed but resorts in actions that transgress the morals of the community. Throughout the play, Odie confesses that the major cause of his decision to betray his close relatives is their decision to relegate him as the other. He joins the State Research Bureau to spy on his brother Wak and father. Odie is driven by bitterness and jealousy to vouch for Wak and his father's detention. The father is detained and killed and Odie has to be haunted by that guilt. When Wak wants to know why Odie did it, he looks at the father's photo and says, "[o]h dear poor Papa. I am making a monkey of myself, am I? Good. Real good (he smashes the portrait," (129). Odie in this passage refers to the incident in the past when he led a strike at the university and the father relegated him further. Odie observes, "[m]y own father never forgave me for it," (37). Witu claimed that Odie had maligned the family's name. By smashing the father's portrait, Odie demonstrates how bitter he is. Odie's self has the semblance to what Zepenic refers to as "sense of emptiness with a painful intensity in form of flashback." (84). Odie is not capable of any constructive conversations with those around him save for recriminations and bitter flashbacks. The self is shattered into anger, fury, bitterness and melancholy and can recall nothing else. When stella raises the question of the inheritance in which Odie betrayed his brother and suggests that Odie should see a psychiatrist, he vindictively responds:

> You can have him for your dinner and piss off to the penitentiary or the psychiatrist. As I said, it is you who needs the little trot. Thought about it for quite some time now. (*bombshell*) Five years to be exact. Since you started going out with Ali. Do you know Major General Ali, Stella? Do you remember him? ...the man everyone knows signed a death warrant for our father. You and him night after night. (29)

As much as Odie's words reveal Stella's act of betrayal to the late father, it is the bitterness and anger in his shattered self that prompt him to say it with the intention to even the score. Ali takes advantage of the family's plight to compel Stella in to an affair. As the dictator's henchman, he wields the powers to propagate impunity in the nation confronted by political animosity and it would be absurd for Stella to refuse. Ali has had Witu murdered and Odie arrested and tortured. Any resistance on Stella's would likewise sign her death warrant.

Odie therefore brings in focus gender othering and its psychological consequences on Stella. He relegates her because she is a woman and faces different challenges contrary to men's. As a woman, the autocratic regime subjects her to sexual exploitation, which Odie refuses to put in consideration. While in school, Mohamed Ali and his soldiers raid Stella's school. Odies says:

> And besides, Stella, do I have to remind you that Ali is a military man? Have you forgotten what his platoon did to you, the nuns and other girls when they raided your school?

> A month before exam time? Drunk and lascivious, they plundered and left behind them a wreckage of piteous things whimpering for life. You, three months in hospital, brutalized and ashamedly expectant. Was it after that, sister, that you threw shame and decency to the jackals? (31)

Odie in this passage demonstrates that many women and girls in the war-torn nation are otherized owing to their sex. The political system sees them as sex objects and also uses rape as an instrument of torture whenever they are found on the wrong. Because Stella's father, Witu and his brother, Wak champion for democracy against the autocratic regime, the regime uses sexual exploitation to punish their female relative. Stella understands that this is the punishment she has to persevere to save his life. Whereas Witu is killed and Odie tortured, Stella is raped and forced into an affair with Ali.

Odie's gender othering affects Stella psychologically. The writer observes, "[t]horoughly crushed, is crouching in a seat covering her face in shame. Spasms of sobbing are visible. Her body is trembling," (31). Stella consistently tells Odie not to remind her of the ordeal to suggest that she did not willingly choose to have an affair with her father's murderer. The unearthing of the scandal results in Stella's "uncontrolled weeping" (31), a symptom of depression. Davison describes Stella's behaviour as antisocial personality disorder (324) because she transgresses the norms by having a romantic relationship with murderer of her father and the enemy of the family. She is therefore a cultural other or a pariah in the Witu family.

Political Otherness and the Fragmented Self: Shattered and Multiple Selves

Characters in Ruganda's *Shreds of tenderness* are stigmatized because of their political ideology. Anthony Downs defines ideology "verbal image of the good society and the chief means of constructing such a society" (96). The 'good society' to some will be realized by dictatorship and to others by democracy. Political otherness in John Ruganda's *Shreds of tenderness* stems from ideological differences between those who believe in dictatorship and those who uphold democracy as a means to Downs' "good society."

As soon as the dictator overthrows the government, characters in *Shreds of tenderness* take sides. Witu and his son Wak take the opposing sides while Odie and Mohamed Ali join the dictator. Taking advantage of the instruments of power, the dictator cleanses the nation off those that stand for democratic principles. They are arrested, detained without trial, tortured and murdered. Having worked for the State Research Bureau (intelligence), Odie is adept in the working of the autocratic regime and lays everything bare in his demented apostrophes. As the play begins, Odie says:

> But now, your case is different. You've refused to talk, haven't you? Refused to co-operate. And that is not very clever of you. Not clever at all. But before long you will start gibbering like a chatterbox. Just you wait and watch. (*He fixes the three ice-trays, puts eyes in them and places the jar on top. The Bunsen burner and the tin of pesticide at the ready...*) (3-4)

The Bunsen burner and ice-trays represent the instruments of torture that the dictator and his henchmen use on those who prop up a divergent ideology. Odie has been spying on such divergent voices and handing them over to the regime. Stella contends that

Wak did not just flee the country to avoid them, but someone informed on him for "talking freely about freedom and the atrocities of the new regime," (14). This assertion reveals Wak's leaning towards democracy contrary to the dictator's totalitarianism. Before his arrest, Wak has planned to give a talk that is inconsistent to the status quo. In a demented hallucination, Odies recounts how he informed on him:

> Isn't he my brother? ...of course he is my brother, sir. Same father, that is. But he is becoming a bit of a nuisance. Threatening to give a talk on democracy and that all. (*Fumbles around in his pockets*). He calls it 'THE INEVITABLE ROAD THAT WILL LEAD US BACK TO DEMOCRACY.' Yes. Always seething with discontent, this brother of mine, like all the rest of his intellectual colleagues...you are right sir. They must be hirelings of foreign forces. Marxist, I should say. Extremely dangerous. Will arouse the public against the government. (123)

Ruganda deliberately uses capitalization to emphasize the root cause of Wak's political marginalisation. He stands for an ideology that is at variant with the status quo: democracy. Driven by his detest for both Wak and Witu, Odie finds a perfect opportunity to wreak a revenge. The autocratic regime uses Marxism as a mask behind which to persecute those who hold divergent views. Luckily, Wak meets the three spies at the university gate and manages to trick them (121). As they follow his directions to Room 213, he rushes home, takes little belongings and flees. Disappointed, Odie and the spies detain Witu over trumped charges and is killed. Given that there is specific charge for Witu's detention, Odie frames, "Pepe spat on the president's portraits," (125). These political prisoners are tortured and murdered in the public by a firing squad.

When Odie, in the pretext of honoring his father presents himself to take his corpse for burial, Mohamed Ali and his henchmen vent all their anger on him. They possibly see him as their opponent's sympathizer and therefore "the other." He suffers the torture that Wak, the democrat would have suffered. Odie says:

> What do you think we are young man? Scavengers? …six months, that is what it almost earned me. For being a dutiful son and demanding to give the old man a decent burial […] day and night. 'Where is you bloody brother? Where is the traitor?' Boots in my groin, butts on my head…and the pincers. If it weren't for you and your master plan… (feigns breakdown). No, man, one doesn't forget such things so easily. (18)

Odie is tortured and castrated by the soldiers for asking for his father's corpse. He remembers the pain he goes through when the pincers are used to cut off his testicles. This was the punishment he and other SRB spies have persistently meted out on all proponents of democracy during the autocratic regime. It is until Stella takes advantage of her affair with Ali that she secures Odie's release. This is what Odie means by "if it weren't for you and your master plan."

As a result of the torture, Odie's psyche disintegrates and he exhibits the presence of other selves in his primary self. Alice Bailey observes as a creative response to trauma, the psyche collapses and the selves the victims paves way for the entrance of those they love or hate. Psychologists refer to the new selves as alter personalities. For, Bailey, this is what results in dissociative identity disorder in traumatized persons (4). Like Takasha who manifests the self of his late Grandfather in Kenzaburo Oe's *Silent Cry*, Odie manifests the presence of his late father and Wak. His late father's self-manifests as a detestable other alongside his primary self through apostrophes. Margaret Ford observes that the addressee of apostrophe is "always a personified abstract quality or inanimate object (27). In other words, Odie speaks to the intimate father within when he does so in various instances in the play.

Renee Kohler-Ryan observes that soliloquy is relevant if it is open to spiritual and human audience. Using the character Macbeth, he argues that his inability to say "amen" after killing Duncan signifies "isolation from communities of the human and the divine," (i). Ryan suggests that soliloquies occur among alienated individuals that are unable to converse with neither God nor fellow man. Ryan's study is invaluable to Odie's experience as Odie resorts to apostrophes to suggest that he is too alienated to converse with neither Wak, Stella nor the divine. He speaks to the late father's alter within. For example, he says, "[g]o away Papa. Leave me alone. I didn't kill your cow with a catapult. It is the ticks in the block and termites in the base," (129). In this utterance, Odie defends himself that he did not betray Wak, but the dictator and his henchmen did it. Witu alter seeks vengeance and it leads Odie by the nose to the Father's persecutors killers to torture and castrate him (18). The alter's major objective is to stop Odie from perpetuating the Witu lineage because of his erroneous decision to betray the biological father and brother. Unaware of his infertility, Wak wonders why Odie has never thought of getting married at forty-four (121). Odie's self also exhibits the presence of those he loves.

As the play begins, he makes a long speech to the jar:

> Your highness. Having a royal nap, Your highness, are you? A royal nap in spite of the shooting and the shelling and the killing outside? [...] YOUR HIGHNESS! Are you deaf, Your mighty highness. Or is it that you have no ear for the onslaughts of man by man? No ear for human cries of woe...no shred of tenderness left in you? The liberation

war is upon our backs and you take time to have a royal nap? (2)

The jar in this exposition stage of the play represents the powers that be, which Odie has obsequiously served for decades. The leader being addressed as "your highness" is the dictator he has revered throughout his service as an SRB spy. While sane audiences see a jar and insects being addressed, Odie addresses the leader he has loved and served many decades until he is overthrown by the liberators. In this apostrophe, he expresses the sense of betrayal in the regimes ineptitude as the liberators advance into the country.

Political othering is also evident in Wak and other migrant characters that flee to foreign nations to escape the dictator's purge. Tanaka Chidora describes the migrant experience as the state of abjection, defined as "forms of existence" that compel one into "shame, disgrace or debasement, rendered beyond the limits of the liveable, denied the warrant of tolerability, accorded purely a negative value," (23). This reiterates exiles in Ruganda's *Shreds of Tenderness*. Wak says:

> But fleeing from your own country...that is another matter man. A different cattle of fish as they say. There is nothing as abominable as being a refugee, let me tell you. Shouted at. Your dignity is lowered. Hell man. It is blight. [...] From the sweeper to the highest official they subtly remind you that you don't belong. You are alien. That word stinks. *Alien. Makwerekwere,* a third rate non-citizen, always associated with hunger and deprivation and cheap labour. (80)

Ruganda demonstrates how the host nation relegates refugees and defines it from the position of exclusion. They remain the lowest of the low and decide to forget about dignity reserved for normal human beings. Wak observes that where citizens are requested, they are growled at; whenever they have a complaint, they are reminded that they are aliens and should shut up. For Fanon, these othering processes affect the selves of characters. Ruganda gives us a number of characters that are relegated by the host nation and how they become victims of the fragmented self.

The first example is the refugee in an imaginary African country that goes to the bar and a citizen, Mr No Fear No Favour casts aspersions on him. The latter clarifies the difference between the self and the other without little consideration of the problems the refugee is passing through. Before, the episode, the narrator observes that othering conditions in exile have reduced the refugee to abject conditions. The narrator says:

> Walks over to a table where a fellow refuge is quietly sipping his beer. A lonely man with a crowded mind in a crowded impersonal city. Nowhere to slip, no food to eat. Wondering what life has in store for him tonight or tomorrow or the day after. What it has in store for his family of five. He is telling us of doors flung in his face countless times. He is now on the brink for the token money from the Joint Refugee Services is running out fast. Lots of ideas are criss-crossing his mind. Suicide is not far from his thoughts. (102)

As Wak explains before this episode, most of the refugees have fled their mother nations because they are perceived as political others by the regime in their mother nations. Defined by exclusion in their host nations, they cannot access meaningful employment and turnout as paupers that solely depend on philanthropists and United Nations High Commission for Refugees. In this passage, the refugee is described as lonely in spite of being married with five children. The self-estrangement arises from relegation by host nation rather than the lack of family and friends. Indeed as he still is wallowing in depression, a citizen, Mr No Fear No Favour storms at the scene and accuses refugees of defiling girls, exploiting women and eating into the economy of the host nation. In countless expletives, the man addresses refugees as mongrels, centipedes and buggers that do nothing save for "fouling the air" in the host nation. He tells the refugee, "[g]o home...Get out you mongrel...I am ordering you to leave," (103). He considers all refugees cowards that refuse to fight for the wellbeing of their nations and migrate as pests that siphon the host nations. He says:

> Why do we let some of these bastards plunder our economy and cause shortage? Why do we let them siphon our maize meal to foreign ports? Where have our coffee and tea gone? To Mongolia or Nicaragua? No sir. Just across the border. Smartly sneaked out under our very noses. *(to the clientele)* And I know some of you are benefitting from this traffic, so don't you provoke me... for in effect, you are aiding these aliens to sabotage our economy, spread veneral diseases and rob our banks in broad daylight. Murders, forgeries, impersonation, hoarding, smuggling...the lot. (Turns to Wak's table) And you there...yes, you! What do you think you are doing with our women? (104-105)

As members of the out-group, immigrants are squarely blamed for all sorts of evil in the host nation. From spreading sexually transmitted diseases, robberies to sapping the host nation's economy. In spite of the psychological trauma the refugee confronts, the host communities do not expect them to visit social places for any entertainment. It is therefore this kind of exclusion that results in depression and other pathological symptoms among refugees. The character in this passage contemplates suicide (102), which in Menninger's view is to "eradicate the detestable Other" (Davison, 252) the dominant group has nurtured in him. The refugee is not just John, Mohamed or Asha their cultural identity demonstrates. He or she is John, Mohamed, Asha and "alien," "murderer," "impersonator," *makwerekwere,* "smuggler" and all the "other" identities stipulated by the mirror that the dominant community creates.

Finally, female refugees experience an infusion of political and gender othering conditions. Ruganda demonstrates the plight of Dr Rugen in the hands of the host nation police officers in an odd episode that confounds the audience. As a non-citizen, her name cannot be articulated by the local police, which accentuate her otherness. When she says she is Dr Rugendarutakaliletirugaruka, the police are shocked and contend that they have never come across such a "tongue twisting name" (97). Although Ruganda does not show pathological effects of othering on Dr Rugen, she possibly cannot experience psychological stability with scorn, sexual harassment and physical assault in the hands of semi-illiterate police officers. Aware of her high academic qualifications embodied in sophisticated English accent, the constable says:

> You are not the type to go around in filthy clothes like the ones you've been wearing for days and days and days. Unwashed, unchanged and generally fouling up God's good atmosphere. And mark you, we mean no harm. For all we know, you may have picked up this terrible stench from the bus or taxi, or train. Your taxi-seat mate may have been the one carrying the substances, but our dog did pick you out. (92)

The description of Dr Rugen in this excerpt gives a clear picture of the degrading conditions that revered academics and other important persons go through after political upheavals. As a political other in the mother nation, Dr Rugen is forced to flee without enough clothes, water, food and other basic necessities. She is now in the hands of semi illiterate local police officers poised to scoff and harass her. Although in most nations policemen are not allowed to search female citizens, they declare their readiness to search her body. When she resists, she is accused of insulting an officer on duty and have her "hold her up by the collar, lifts her up in mid-air till she is dangling like a marionette," (93). The assault and blackmail continues until Dr Rugen feigns to be a victim of HIV AIDS. Perhaps it is the coping strategies that Dr Rugen possesses that save her from pathological consequences of political otherness.

Othering and the Fragmented Self: Ideological Relegation and Pathology in David Mulwa's *Inheritance*

Ideological differences form the basis of othering in David Mulwa's play *Inheritance* such that the family as the basic unit of society is split along these differences with catastrophic consequences on Kutula nation. Mulwa shows how the conflict between Marxism and capitalism that pervaded many nations in the last half of the twentieth century entrenched political othering in African states. The West superintended the capitalistic philosophy and East, Marxism. To Western thinkers, Marxists became the other and Eastern thinkers did not spare othering those that embraced capitalistic ideals. It is confounding how the first family in Mulwa's *Inheritance* turns into a battleground of the two rival ideologies with King Kutula vouching for Marxism while the son goes into bed with capitalists from Western nations. While Kutula exults in laying the foundation to self-reliance, contentment, humility and economic independence, his son Lacuna seethes with fury over his choice of ideology. He therefore see his father as the other in a region where most nations take the path of capitalism as propped by the British colonizers.

Synopsis of Mulwa's *Inheritance*

Mulwa's *inheritance* is the story of King Kutula XV, his son Lacuna and Sangoi the adoptive daughter and how their ideological differences play out in the politics of a fictitious African nation, Kutula. From the outset, King Kutula rejects capitalistic ideology with its imperialistic attributes and opts for socialist way of thinking. He supports the struggle of the peasants against dominant colonialist bourgeoisie class. He warns Governor Thorne MacKay that unless the whites leave Kutula Colony they will continue to die in the hands of the restive peasants. Governor Mackay is so infuriated that he describes King Kutula as Communist that can only eradicated through substitution by his lascivious son after independence. Through a careful combination of economic manipulation and political chicanery, Mackay and Menninger succeed to carry out the king's assassination and replace him with the lecherous Lacuna. With promises of financial rewards, he bows to the wicked request to poison his father and introduces in Kutula a capitalistic regime. With scorn and arrogance, Lacuna tramples on his father's philosophy of humility and contentment and institutes an autocratic regime with little regard for the poor. From the outset, Lacuna is intolerant to criticism and those with divergent views are assigned the role of the other. Sangoi, his adoptive sister is relegated and constantly described in derogatory terms. Leaders of the civil rights movement such as Bengo serve long terms in prison and Judah Zen Mello and Tamina that refuse to adhere to Lacuna's wishes become objects of political othering. In spite of the constant hypocrisy, Lacuna understands that he has transgressed cultural norms by killing his own father. The constant guilt prompts him to recall the father's curse through flashbacks that are disastrous to his mental health. As a child, his father favoured Sangoi and relegated him from any matters concerning succession. Age othering therefore contributes to Lacuna's fragmented self. As the revolution gather's pace, its astonishing how Lacuna demonstrates narcissistic tendencies. He brags that he is still popular and the people cherish him. As he is seducing Lulu a girl young enough to be his daughter, the revolutionaries overpower the security operatives and overthrow him.

Age Othering and Pathology: Fragmented Antagonist in Mulwa's *Inheritance*

One aspect that affects the antagonist Lacuna in Mulwa's *inheritance* is his father's decision to relegate him at an early age. Like Odie in *Shreds of Tenderness,* Lacuna is disliked by his father, King Kutula XV. When the play begins, the audience comes across the King visiting Governor MacKay palace with his adopted daughter Sangoi. This is a symbolic gesture that signifies his readiness to leave his position for Sangoi. Whereas he speaks passionately about Sangoi at the palace, King Kutula does not mention Lacuna even in passing. Menninger, the Governor's Christian advisor comments that Sangoi is always at the King's side and she replies that she has to be near him to learn (13). In an altercation with Governor Mackay about education of Africans, King Kutula contends that he has no qualms about it. He says, "[t]ake our children and train them beginning with my daughter, Princess Sangoi," (12). Throughout the King's conversations, he ignores the word "adoptive" in relation to Sangoi probably because he sees her as a perfect substitution to his son Lacuna.

Kutula's closeness with Sangoi suggests that he has neglected his son completely. He does not bother mentor him as parent should. Menninger reveals in a conversation with Governor Macay:

> Kutula has an only child. One *legitimate* child: Prince Lacuna Kasoo. Sangoi was picked from the gutter- an orphan. And

she is not our worry…a thoroughly debased moral reprobate! Out of loins of this King of Truths, comes the mud that will see him home…my observations tell me that the boy has the mind of a perfect noodle. He is an ingenious greedy rascal that's utterly devoid of human feelings. Loves his pleasure. Nero and Carigula rolled into one ambitious mould- would throw his mother to the Lions given the chance to become Caesar Augustus. (15)

The reader is confounded that King Kutula has only one biological child, but behaves in absolutely contrary manner to his highly cherished principles such as humility, contentment and integrity. As much as Lacuna has individual weaknesses, his father's constant mentorship would have contributed in shaping him into a responsible adult. However, Kutula gives up on him and resorts in preparing Sangoi for the inheritance. Menninger describes him as silly, lascivious hedonist that can kill for anything possibly because of his father's neglect. While to the King Lacuna's ill character arises from personal weaknesses, age othering is the real culprit. In a conversation with Sangoi, Lacuna demonstrates how his father's neglect affects him. In an expletive, he suddenly growls when Sangoi underscores the need to appease the ancestors: "I forgot you learned to prattle with him in his makeshift court (*suddenly vicious*). You did get my orders, not so?" (56). This conversation reveals the jealousy that his father's othering nurtured in Lacuna. He develops a psychological condition that Heinz Kohut and Earnest Wolf refer to it as the unburdened self. It is a self that confronts trauma without any support and develop weak self-soothing capabilities that protect normal individuals from being traumatized by the spreading of emotions. The self is neglected in early life and therefore experiences the surroundings as hostile. The victims therefore dream of living in a poisoned atmosphere or surrounded by swarms of hornets, they complain of noise and unpleasant odours and maintain a general attitude of irritability and suspiciousness (417). Lacuna's expletive in the above episode demonstrates the constant irritability typical of the unburdened self. Kohut and Wolf's argument links Lacuna's pathological symptoms to childhood, which confirms the father's neglect during childhood. He does not stand Sangoi's advice. When she tries to question his order on the relocation of people from Bukelenge Valley, he contends:

> Tell them I have not forgotten that on the day of my coronation, their foul breath wafted about my ears for me to step down, so a leader of their choice can take my place. I heard their teaching beneath that madness, Sangoi but I forgave you. I forgave you because you once called my father, Father though nobody knows your mother. I am the only legitimate heir to Leadership, Sangoi and deep down, my people know my ancestry, lineage and my unquestionable majesty...take care my one time sister- take care. (87)

This monologue demonstrates the nexus between Lacuna's pathological self and his father's favoritisms for Sangoi. After his death, the people of Kutula are aware that the departed King had mentored Sangoi to inherit him. They therefore demand that she be allowed to take leadership. As earlier discussed, Lacuna has always been out of the picture as the father dislikes his character in spite of being the legitimate heir to the throne. With financial and moral support from Daniel Goldstein and Menninger, he eliminates his father and usurps the throne. But given the crude means by which the takeover is effected, Lacuna confronts guilt and other disastrous aspects of pathology.

One such element is the catastrophic flashback of his infamous act and the father's curse. Christopher Ball and Jennifer Little aver that such a flashback confirms how the character's life has been disrupted (175). In a conversation with Goldstein, Lacuna descends into a hallucinatory flashback that reveals the haunting ordeal that has resulted in his current pathological condition. He says:

> And then it happened- I had to do it... not that I hate him. No he is my father and I love him. I must do it for the future. ...Menninger say so...standing in the courtyard... "A little powder in his tea, tasteless beneath the sugar." My father likes sugar...his weakness... "I've brought you your favourite tea, my father." And he's... that childlike smile, trusting heart...I give him ...the cup...is my hand trembling? He looks into my eyes...he drinks; ...his body shudders...that wince on his face...doubles up in pain...my beloved son, What is this that you have done to me?...he took long to die...Daniel, and I killed him. (68-69)

The tragic ordeal that Lacuna effects as a retaliation against his father disrupts his life to the extent that he loses grip of his mental health. The confession that "he had to do it" carries two meanings: he was compelled by the age othering- the father's favouring of Sangoi and Menninger's incitement. If he did not hate the father then the true object of spite was Sangoi who he had to subdue in the savage wrangle for power. The flashback arises from the pre-conscious as he contravenes the rational demands by releasing perilous secrets such that Goldstein warns him. Expressions such as "he took long to die," depict the anguish Lacuna undergoes as a result of the ensuing guilt all these years. Even when he pretends to remember his father through grandiose ceremonies, the guilt disrupts him. He gets agitated when Sangoi recites the Lord's Prayer asking for the forgiveness of sins. She as to stop because she notices Lacuna disturbed; he "sighs with relief" (54) when she ends the prayer midway.

King Kutula's last words come in devastating flashbacks that threaten Lacuna's sanity. Before he died after Lacuna's poisoning, King Kutula uttered, "when the waters spill across my unguarded grave," (89) then Lacuna's reign would come to the end. The waters represent the revolution in which the people of Kutula rise against Lacuna's leadership. As Bengo arranges a peaceful demonstration of Millions of dove and twig carrying Kutulans, it becomes clear to Lacuna's henchmen that the regime cannot survive. Lacuna is compelled to ask for the forgiveness he has always refused. In an apostrophe, he tells his father:

> My father, lay not my sin across my doorstep and let your son serve your children for yet another term. *(he kneels)* See only humility upon my bended knee. See only penitence and let the bridge stay in place....only this once and I shall... (89)

The apostrophe is the summit his fragmentation as he descends into the preconscious to converse with his father's self within. The prayer for humility is answered by news of the swelling revolution and replication of fear and pride that dominate his self forthwith. The father's prophecy accentuates the fear. He tells Malipoa, the seer, "[t]he flood! Yes, that flood. The Flood my father warned against," (92). He defies the seer's advice to stop his advances on Lulu, kills her father to have her full possession and declares himself a god. His lust for Lulu can no longer permit him to consult the ancestors. He tells the seer:

> The silent ones had better remain silent in their world of the dead. ..You priests and preachers pretend communion with the unseen blackmailing me to servitude all this time. I am I... he who now holds all power. And you shall serve me as you serve your gods. Go fetch the girl. Before sunset,

I shall appear before the people as their new saviour...
(116).

Lacuna assumes absolute power over the natural and supernatural to gratify his lust for sex. By saying he is "I am," he tries to declare himself Jehovah as expounded in the Book of Exodus. He rejects any other truth except what matters in his own eyes. Scholars refer to these egoistical attributes as symptomatic of narcissistic personality disorder. Richard Bootzin and Joan Acocella observe that narcissistic personality disorder is characterized by grandiose sense of self-importance with periodic feelings of inferiority (264). Heinz Kohut avers that these personalities will brag about their talents and achievements and predict for themselves great success (254). Bootzin and Acocella add that the self-love in narcissists is accompanied with a fragile self-esteem causing them to check constantly how they are regarded by others and react with rage or despair in response to criticism (264). This is Lacuna's case whenever he is criticized in Mulwa's *Inheritance*. He brags of being a better manager than his father, but when Robert and Goldstein analyse the economic health of Kutula they find it wanting. In the mining sector, the output has declined by fifteen per cent (71), the industry has political sycophants and tribesmen instead of professionals (71) and most of the loans have either been misused or deposited in private accounts in Canada, Luxemburg and Switzerland (111). When Robert and Goldstein question him, he retorts that he is a leader and had to buy a plane to elevate his status so the subjects "look up to me," (72). When the two whitemen withdraw the money from his accounts, he reacts furiously by ordering their detention without trial. Lacuna also superintends the sacking and subsequent torture of Judah Zen Mello when he questions his directive to kill his brother, Bengo. Sangoi tells Zen Mello's wife, Tamina that Lacuna will never tolerate criticism (43) and is also a victim of paranoia. She says, "[a] mind like his thinks nothing but enemies, dissenters, contradictions and shadows in the dark," (44). Lulu refers to his self-importance when he kills her father and insists on marrying her. Lacuna demonstrates his narcissistic attributes when he tells Lulu, "I am all the people now...when I breathe, they breathe. I am their god I am their past and the only future they will know," (120). Lulu questions him why he thinks life is only about him. She asserts, "[i]t is all you, you and you! You don't care about anyone else," (120). Indeed as the revolution gathers pace, the narcissistic tendencies worsen; he sacks all state officers and civil servants and becomes the sole leader to run government. He says:

All citizens remain indoors- curfew from dawn to dusk and around the clock. All positions abolished except army ranks. Councillors abolished. Ministers abolished. Directors abolished. Principals abolished. Teachers and all the pupi...keep those. I'll need leaders when I choose to die on this throne.

He can no longer trust the running of government in the hands of others owing to the paranoia gnawing at his self. It is absolutely shattered and lacks the unity to enable him reason and lead people. Lacuna is therefore a psychological wretch owing to othering conditions that pervade Kutula since his childhood. Although most critics associate insanity and the fragmented self in the oppressed, Mulwa suggests that they are likewise aspects of the oppressor because of age othering in the family unit.

Political Othering and the Shattered Self: Disorders of the Self at the Marginal Space

The focus of this subsection is the impact of political relegation of characters in Mulwa's *Inheritance* on their selves. The rampant political persecution of characters owing to their ideological principles results in psychological strains that curtail their normal existence and well ness. Judah Zen Melo is party loyalist that rejects his brother's rebellion and tows party lines. Whereas his younger brother Bengo starts a revolutionary movement to oppose Lacuna's autocratic and avaricious policies, Zen Mellow remains loyal for his self-preservation. Enraged by Bengo's opposition, Lacuna resolves that Zen Melo, the elder brother should be the means through which to eliminate him. One evening during a party, Lacuna shoves aside and they have a conversation:

> Judah Zen Melo, my son in politics, do you love me?
> Of course, leader, of course
> Enough to confront even my greatest enemies and humble them to the dust?
> -indeed Your Excellency
> Ah, good. You will surely prove it to me. I have a thorn in my political side, Judah, my boy and I want you to pluck it out, then rub my paining side with the red balm of loyalty-his red blood upon your hand.
> And who is this my, Leader?
> A man called Romanus Bengo, your brother, the communist. (23)

The last of Lacuna's utterance comes as confounding revelation to Zen Melo because "the thorn" in question is his younger brother. The Leader expects of Melo to shed his brother's blood for self-preservation and political privileges, which he finds outrageous. Melo goes into silence, musters courage and replies in the negative, "[n]o, I cannot betray my own blood, and the mother who bore me and him," (23). He remains faithful to the sacred bond ascribed between him and Bengo. Forthwith, the Lacuna regime assigns him the role of the political other and is subjected to persecution and torture characteristic of the other in Kutula. Political othering begins when Lacuna retorts, "THEN THAT IS ALL, JUDAH ZEN MELO! THAT-IIS- ALL!" (23). This capitalized utterance suggests that Zen Melo belongs to the other Marxist faction under Bengo's leadership and should have nothing to do with Lacuna. In the Leader's perspective, the other should be subjected to severe persecution or death. He sends his henchman to have Melo tortured. Tamina says, "[t]hey dumped his mangled body at our government house doorstep," (23). He was sacked from his position in government, his coffee farm taken by Chipande and his wife Tamina began seeking for petty jobs as he and sons went out to seek for employment. Tamina says:

> Where are the cars I used to drive? The good government house we lived in? My coffee farm in Bukelenge Mountains? All gone. Now I must pick coffee for Chipande on the farm that he had me sell to him for peanuts. (24)

As a marked family, they are reduced to abjection to serve as a warning to any other party member that refuses the leader's direction. Zen Mello travels away from home to seek for odd jobs in the country. He becomes a security officer and after bribing the manager, he is promoted as a machine operator (38). As a result of the political othering, Judah's family exhibits various strains of the fragmented self and disorders of the self.

Firstly, Zen Melo's wife Tamina and daughter, Lulu are constantly depressed. They are constantly irritable and threaten to fight with each other or others. When Bengo is released and pays Tamina a visit, she is infuriated by his presence and insolently shows him the seat saying, "[t]he chair are there…" (17) and proceeds to stir "the pan with increasing hostility," (17). After Bengo has his seat, Tamina goes into a long flashback that traces the fall of the family from grace following Bengo's detention. Scholars contend that flashbacks are symptomatic of psychological disruption of such persons (Ball and Little 175). Tamina's self is therefore altered by political othering that she has to talk about past ordeals as a therapy. When Bengo encourages her that Kutula will change, he retorts, "[t]ake your mad ideas elsewhere. First it was Zen Melo. Then it will be this house once the octopus learns you have come here. *(she takes a plate, angrily covers the food on the pan. An awkward solid silence)*" (24). Tamina rudely chases Bengo away given the present psychological trauma.

Her daughter Lulu comes in the house and she exhibits depressive symptoms because of the abject poverty she experiences. She has been sent home for fees, which the parents do not have. When the mother wants to know why she has come home early, she gets angry: "Questions! Questions! Questions…*aghs, ts,* and "(25 The school administration is very strict to expedite Lacuna's capitalistic philosophy that strives to replace King Kutula's socialism. He therefore tells administrators, "[n]o free things any more. The holiday is over," (27). The school therefore demands among other things tuition fee balance: two thousand, construction fund (second perimeter fence): three thousand; examination fee (paper and marking): two thousand, (26-27). The exaggerated fees balances trigger depression in Tamina and Lulu owing to their poverty political othering has set the family.

Worried and scared, Tamina descends into lamentations:

> Just tell them I can't pay. Every morning I wake up before cockcrow and pick those coffee beans until sunset. I walk all this distance, back home and nobody has paid me for

extra work. (*she looks long at the paper lost in thought, her brow in her let palm. Pause. The paper falls to the ground*). (27)

The pessimistic tone in this passage demonstrates the hopelessness characteristic of depression. The financial demands made by the school are inconsistent to the class in which the family is. They have lost their former position because they are the political other and Tamina is sincere when she describes her current class. However hard she strives, her current job with its meagre pay cannot pay the exorbitant balances. The depression leads to absent mindedness and the paper falls.

Infuriated by the mother's resignation, Lulu's depression emerges through similar lamentations and profanity. She blurts:

> Poor! Always in fear. Fear that the rains will fail. Fear that tomorrow you'll fall sick and lose your job. I want to be above all this…this uncertainty…this gasping and holding our breath each moment Chenko's radio up at the village broadcasts the news. (30)

The parents' failure to pay school fees bespeak of her class otherness, which emanates from political othering of the family. She possibly juxtaposes the family's situation in the pre and post political persecution. Her anger is immeasurable as she casts aspersions upon the current conditions of desperation. Lulu aspires to be a doctor and above the poverty line that the regime has set for her father, Zen Melo, the uncle Bengo and mother Tamina. But that is a goal superlatively unattainable in the current political set up. She too is well aware of it. It is not surprising when she informs the mother that she is prepared to give herself to men to obtain the school fees to meet the cost of her education (31). Her mother Tamina reprimands her for adopting a philosophy that Lacuna, the lascivious leader, and his henchmen already exploit to extract sexual pleasure from desperate girls in Kutula.

Lulu's depression also exhibits itself through hypercriticism particularly at the divine. Although raised to revere piety, Lulu turns her heart away from religion and directs expletives at the supernatural. Asked how she will ascend the social ladder, she inverts or doctors Biblical verses saying "[e]verything is possible with God or man," (30). This is an expletive that implies that she would use unscrupulous means including prostitution to get rich. When Tamina reprimands her, more profanity breaks forth:

> It's true. Mama Reverend Sangoi used to teach us that only with God was anything possible. But just look at this dry dusty valley. Is God here? [...] then I don't believe in Him anymore [...] how can He live in a place like this? We are alone, Mama. Alone. You have prayed since I was small and only the dusty winds answer you. No. I shall do it myself if He won't do it. (30)

Lulu is overwhelmed by anxiety that sets off the angry tone of this passage. She also feels that they are too lonely to face the future forthwith. The subsequent sadness and hopelessness prompt her to rebel against all the religious teaching she has received from Reverend Sangoi and her mother. Lulu is alienated from her current conditions, which is self-alienation. George Hegel defines self-alienation as a separation between the essence and its condition. Hegel adds that it is through culture that the individual gives form to itself. He writes, "[t]his individuality moulds itself by culture to what it inherently is, and only by so doing is it then something per se and possesses of concrete existence" (419, 515). By reneging against the religious norms of the family, Lulu transgresses the culture through which she should be formed. As the mother threatens to punish her, she says, "I don't want this life!I don't, I don't!" Tamina starts abdicating her parental role in relation to her because of her profanity. She maintains pathological relationship with Tamina throughout the play. When Tamina warns her against honouring Lacuna's invitation, she rebels again (99) and ends up entrapped in Lacuna's wiles at the palace.

Finally, Judah Zen Melo experiences a disorder of the self as a result of political othering. Zen Melo rejects his Christian principles and resorts to alcoholism. Kohut and Wolf refer to this disorder of the self under stimulated self and define it as a self in which patients lack vitality and experience themselves as boring, apathetic and are experienced by others the same way (418). Desperate for happiness, the individuals stimulate themselves by addictive promiscuous activities, perversions, gambling, drug and alcohol induced excitement and lifestyle characterized by hyper sociability.

Having suffered for months in search for casual jobs after being sacked and tortured by Lacuna regime, Melo takes to alcoholism to find ephemeral excitement. After being promoted to the machine operator's post, he is overworked. He fears that if he rests, someone else will take his place. When he visits home the first time after getting the job, he says:

I am a man, *oi*! A man and I am drunk. (*sings*)
You say I sin when I drink my own money. You say I am a fool because money goes down my throat in these hard times. *Shaddup*! (hic) didn't ask you why I drink, I know! Me: Zen-Melo! Baptized Judah, the Warrior lion of Judah! (sings). Hey Rev Sangoi, you're a good woman, but *wacha wewe* –no more sweet words, eh? You can't fool me. Not anymore. Because I won't look up at the sky. I refuse to see the stars! (sings) 'you say the spirit left me…therefore…. (47)

This dramatic monologue constitutes Melo's attempt to excite the self that has been alienated by prolonged persecution and victimisation. He vows that he will neither practice Christian principles nor depend on the divine because of the traumatizing economic and political realities. Rev Sangoi is the epitome of Christianity in Kutula and she is therefore warned to keep away.

Before this monologue, he recounts how he had to attend evening sessions in bars to bribe managers to get the promotion (36). After getting the job, he works without rest in the fear that another person will take the job. As a result, his self is so alienated that he cannot maintain intimacy with his wife without drinking. Through ambiguity, the playwright suggests Zen Melo struggles to have normal erections when he refuses to go to bed with his wife because "the machine" (39) will not work. The "machine" in this context refers to his manhood that has undergone dysfunction as result of traumatic experiences rather than the one he operates in Lacuna's company.

The writer's reference to the bar as "up there" is a reference to Laing's concept of the fragmented self that retreats from normal life to the mind. Laing observes that the self avoids all participation in physical life and focuses only on activities that are purely mental (71). Melo dislikes the poverty in his home: daughter's school fees arrears, small hut, landlessness and troubled wife and prefers to go, drink and deceive his mind. Benard Hart refers to drunkenness as that typical of Melo as phantasy. For Hart, people may find it extremely difficult to cope with painful realities of life and create an imaginary world to obtain counterfeit fulfilment. Such people content themselves by building of pleasant mental world in which to obtain imaginary fulfilment (155). Melo creates an alcoholic world from which he enjoys a fake paradise, for example, he makes several references to his being king and the wife, queen (48, 49). Between the brags, he descends back to bouts of depression and whimpers, "[s]et us free o God!...let my people go!" This cry for freedom draws the audience attention to the fact that alcoholism is just a sickness Melo resorts to with no tangible impact to his political and economic realities.

Conclusion

From the foregoing discussion, it is apparent that the nexus between strands of otherness and fragmentation of the self is not a preserve of the novel. Many playwrights have delved into the subject to ascertain that political, class and age marginalisation deals a heavy blow on the psyche of characters. Both Ruganda and Mulwa demonstrate how marginalisation of groups in different ways results in strains of self fragmentation such as depression and disorders of the self. One interesting aspect is how othering at the family level with reference to age severely affects the mental health of characters such as Odie and Lacuna.

Chapter Three

Otherness and Madness in African Fiction

Introduction

In the previous chapter, focus has been on analysis of the nexus between otherness and the fragmented self in contemporary African fiction. In this chapter, we are concerned with the nexus between diverse strands of otherness and madness, particularly schizophrenia. This chapter takes Frantz Fanon's trajectory in demonstrating how systematic negation of the other alters the self of characters and drives them to symptoms of insanity such as delusions and hallucinations. Although the fragmented self is quite disabling, it does not alienate the victim completely from reality as is the case in madness. Gerald Davison and colleagues cite the following words form a mad patient:

> When I'm psychotic, I feel like I'm a disembodied soul. I'm in contact with fairy kings, delusionary people. Sometimes I'm not even aware there are normal people around me, I am so caught up in fantasy ... some time like when I thought I was brother Michael, Michael the Archangel, I thought I had the power to heal people. (326)

Sandy, a thirty-seven year old schizophrenic, says the above words to give a hint into the nature of clinical madness. It is evident that strains of the fragmented self discussed in previous sections are not as disabling as Sandy's condition. Those around her experience a patient, but Sandy deludes herself as a noble dining with kings; she is the Biblical Angel, Michael with supernatural powers to heal all ill people around her. The onlookers wonder why she cannot heal herself first. From this example, Davison defines schizophrenia as a mental disorder characterized by severe disturbances in thought, emotion and behaviour. The person's thinking is illogical, perception is faulty accompanied with inappropriate affect and disturbances in motor activity (324). John Csernansky refers to acute schizophrenic phase as psychosis (109). It is therefore a severe degree of schizophrenia. Examples of schizophrenics in literary works are Bertha, Rochester's Creole wife in Bronte's *Jane Eyre*. Rochester narrates his experiences to demonstrate the psychotic nature of his wife. He tells Jane, "[t]he lunatic is both cunning and malignant; she has never failed to take advantage of her guardian's temporary lapses; once to secrete the knife with which she stabbed her brother…in the first of these occasions, she perpetrated the attempt to burn me in bed" (307). Csernansky singles this out as agitation, a state of heightened emotional arousal typical of psychosis (110). In African literature, Ezeulu is one such an example; Achebe writes, "[b]ut in this final act of malevolence, proved merciful. It allowed Ezeulu in his last days to live in the haughty splendour of a demented high priest and spared him the knowledge of the final outcome," (233). Achebe implies that Ezeulu wandered around shouting in exaggerated sense of self-importance, which is grandiose delusion typical of paranoid schizophrenia. There is also Othello whose psyche collapses when Iago, the white junior officer schemes to bring him to grass because he is black. It is the contention of this chapter that clinical madness in literary characters stems from strands of otherness: Othello confronts racial otherness since Caucasians hate moor in Europe; Bertha's otherness is three-pronged: racial, cultural and gender, a Creole married to a white man and Ezeulu's case stems from cultural otherness- the clash between African and Western culture. This chapter will focus on the nexus between Otherness and schizophrenia in characters in Farah's *Gifts*, and *Close Sesame* and El Saadawi's *God Dies by the Nile*.

Gender Othering and Schizophrenia in Farah's *Gifts* and El Saadawi's *God Dies by the Nile*

In *Gifts,* Farah returns to his criticism of Somali traditional norms that immure women in the marginal space and affect their psyche. Like *The Crooked Rib,* the novelist highlights the psychological consequences of gender othering on Duniya, Fariida, Yussur, Hibo and other female characters. Although the title gifts has been interpreted by critics as the economic aid from donor nations as a result of the political upheavals in Somalia, in this chapter the title *Gifts* is derived from Duniya's rejection of presents given by men as a gateway to patriarchal domination. She therefore rejects any gifts offered by men and tells her daughter Nasiiba to refrain from taking all monetary gifts from men because the gift is a way of bolstering class othering of women (26). She also tells Abshir to resist every kind of domination including being given something (242). Duniya wishes that her epitaph reads, "[H]ere lies Duniya who distrusted givers." The epitaph demonstrates how men take advantage of their economic positions to relegate women and girls in subordinate positions thereby affecting their psyches. As privilege, the men either marry off or marry very young girls. Duniya is given to the old man Zubair by her father. Abshir tells Duniya that were she a boy, he would not have been married off to a spouse as old as their grandmother and may have received a scholarship to the University of her Choice (242). Duniya therefore becomes a victim of early marriage and inability to achieve dreams because of her feminine gender. In Saadawi's *God Dies by the Nile* is a harrowing tale of the Mayor's patriarchal treatment of women and girls in the colonial Egypt. Debilitated by patriarchal religious institutions, Zakeya's and her female relations are helpless before the omnipotent Mayor who maintains predatory attitude towards

Zakeya's granddaughters. Her inability to protect them has devastating consequences on her psyche and suffers incessant psychological disturbances that are misconstrued as demonic possession. Her visits to sheikhs for traditional treatments yield no results possibly because the causes of her insanity stems from gender othering, which remains intact.

Synopsis of Farah's *Gifts* and El Saadawi's *God Dies by the Nile*.

Farah's *Gifts* is the story of Duniya, a young Somali nurse that falls in love with Basaaso and suffers gruesome psychological alienation because of her ambivalence towards men. Men are the object of her love and hate. Duniya has always disliked how men dominate her society and associates them with oppression that endangers the very existence of women. But she also sees them as fathers, brothers and husbands. She hates Taariq, her second husband, Shiriye her arrogant half-brother and Qaasim, her brother in law. On the contrary, she loves her brother Abshir and Basaaso her husband. This vacillation between the love and hate for men results in psychological alienation that drives her into noontime reveries and physical isolation. In some instances, the narrator reveals that Duniya's female self has been substituted by male selves because of the othering conditions she and fellow women have lived in. She experiences intimacy mishaps that manifest through two divorces, but finally finds love in Basaaso. He abandons women such as Waaberi that solely stick closer because of his gifts and opts for the independent Duniya (222). As the story comes to a close, Duniya's heart reaches a still point; she finds peace in her love for Basaaso because it is not based on the traditional binary where the man is the giver and usurps powers to relegate the woman. Basaaso becomes the man whose odour Duniya loves and kisses as the world waits to listen to their love story. Set in a beautiful sleepy village, Kafr El Teen, El Saadawi's *God Dies by the Nile* is a story of a tyrannical corrupt Mayor who takes advantage of his political power and patriarchal traditions to abuse women and girls. The mayor leads the community in perpetuating practices that treat women like slaves. As the novel begins, Kaffrawi reports to Zakeya that her niece, Naffisa has disappeared from Kafr El Teen. As the story unfolds, it becomes clear that the Mayor's lustful advances are squarely to blame for the plight of many girls including Kaffrawi's daughters, Neffisa and Zeinab. He has raped Zeinab before and when she passes by, he looks at "her firm rounded buttocks pressing up against the long gabaleya from behind" (18). He gives Sheikh Zahran instructions to order Kaffrawi to surrender Neffisa; when she refuses, Zahrani advises Kaffrawi that "girls and women never do what they are told unless men beat them" (27). Neffisa runs away the Mayor accuses Elwau of wooing her and he is beaten to death. Besieged by many instances of gender othering, including her late husband's acts of violence, Zakeya's psyche collapses and has to visit sheikhs in search for healing. Her visit to El Sayeda Mosque does not yield any solutions and she gives up on prayer. Hajj Ismail claims that she is possessed by demons. After her son Galali is arrested for planning to Marry Neffisa, Zakeya plunges into her lucid moments, picks a hoe and strikes the Mayor dead.

Gender Othering and Pathology: multiple Selves and Madness in *Gifts* and *God Dies by the Nile*

> We are born cursed…born cursed from the time our mothers bring us into the world till the shrouds are put on us…they begin to shape us to our cursed end…when we are tiny things in shoes and socks. We sit with our little feet drawn up under us in the window, and look at the boys in their happy play. We want to go. Then loving hand is laid on us, 'little one, you cannot go. …your face will burn and your nice white dress be spoiled.' (Showalter, 199-200)

Marginality with regard to sex differences between men and women is ingrained within parenting and general bringing up of male and female children. The above quotation from Elaine Showalter's *A Literature of their Own* attests to this gender stereotyping that paves way to gender othering of girls from an early age. Whereas the boys enjoy liberties at play and socialization, girls are compelled to remain concealed from the public space because of their sex difference. Some differences are so stigmatized that the feminine gender is viewed as "cursed". Female characters in Farah's *Gifts* and Saadawi's *God Dies by the Nile* experience what Showalter describes as "cursed" through the undue domination by men of which traumatic consequence is either clinical symptoms of schizophrenia or madness. In Farah's *Gifts* the heroine Duniya, Zubair's wife, Fariida, Yussur and Hibo are victims of gender othering and exhibit symptoms of madness.

Zubair is a wealthy man without regard for women and after having seven children with the first wife seeks out beautiful virgins to gratify his lust (35). The narrator reveals the betrayal Zubair's wife experiences in his hands:

When she was a little bigger, Duniya heard the story of how Zubair's former wife fell in love with a Jinni, whom she bore several children. Zubair had been married to her for almost twenty years with grown-up sons and daughters who had by then given them grandchildren; and he was busy courting the affections of a much younger woman. (36)

It is Zubair's infidelity that prompts Zubair's wife's eccentric disappearance from her matrimonial home. In spite of her labour to give him seven children, he pay her back by seeking a polygamous marriage arrangement. Ngobizwe Ngema observes that the institution of polygamy is tantamount to gender othering. She writes:

> It is clear that to some people this may be perceived as a blatant discrimination against women. This is partly supported by the fact that in Zulu culture, a man who has multiple sexual partners or wives is known as "isoka" while the man with one or no sexual partner, *"isishimane"*, a derogatory term used to label someone with one partner. A woman with more than one sexual partner is regarded as *"isifebe"* a derogatory term. (11)

In this passage, men are permitted to have many sexual partners, but woman that does that is stigmatized. This is why they refereed in a derogatory manner as *Isifebe* while the men are appraised. Whereas The Zulu community gives a space for polyandry, Zubair's community usurps religious precepts to deny women such a space; subsequently they are locked in disharmonious and unequal marriage relationships. Perhaps this is why Farah does not mention Zubair's wife's name to reiterate Simone De Bouvour's assertions:

> Woman is a relative being. She is defined and differentiated with reference to man and not he with reference to her. She

is the incidental, the inessential, as opposed to the essential. He is the subject, he is absolute- she is the Other. (15-16)

The woman has therefore no identity of her own and most times takes the name of the husband after marriage: Mrs. Harry, Mrs. Wafula or Mrs. Kinyanjui. Zubair's community denies his wife an identity of her own besides assigning her the child bearing role. Zubair is the subject and the wife is the other that cannot question his decision to court a beautiful younger lover.

The same circumstances surround Duniya's experience since it is absurd for her male relatives to capitalize on her infantile joke to marry her off to old Zubair. At the age of seventeen, on his deathbed, Duniya's father gives her in marriage to old Zubair without consulting her and as custom demands, she cannot transgress "the wishes of the dead and the elderly" (38). The narrator writes:

> An intimation of his imminent death that day made Duniya's father speak his last feverish words. He decided to offer as he put it, 'a gesture of kind violence' to his friend and peer Zubair. Would Duniya please take him as her lawful husband? The curse of it was that no one else was there, only Duniya's mother. And Duniya accepted to do her mother's bidding... (38)

In spite of the sanitization of the father's utterance as the "father's last wishes, this episode reveals that the girl in Duniya's society is a material gift that is transferrable from one person to another. She is just a commodity the father gives to his friend to leave a legacy of generosity before he dies. This reiterates Manase Chiweshe's assertion that through some African traditions, [w]omen's bodies are commoditized and they become the site of complex interactions of patriarchy, power and politics. It is the body and particularly the vagina and the womb which is the physical space for sex and reproduction which is intrinsically transferred from the father to the groom (231). For Chiweshe, Duniya's father is giving his friend the private part a gift as a gesture of friend friendship. Oddly enough this marriage is birthed in jest. Zubair turns out as Duniya's first husband whose betrothal begins as an infantile joke by the young Duniya that she would like to ride Old Zubair's horse. When he asks what he would receive in return, the little girl says she would marry him and old Zubair receives the news with pleasure (35).

The second marriage was characterized by a selfish husband that did not think a woman needed sexual satisfaction. Taariq, Duniya's husband, craves sex whether Duniya desires it or not. Duniya says, "Taariq wanted it nightly," (105) regardless of whether she has periods or not. Worse still, Taariq just cares about his animal satisfaction because, "he came at the point when she started to climb the ladder of her own pleasure," (105). Taariq tends to have an inherent contempt for women such that he cannot control his sexual feelings to satisfy the wife. Furthermore, parental responsibility in Taariq's perspective is the role of the "other" gender and he would rather move from one drinking spree to the other than look after the children. In a flashback, the narrator associates Taariq with, "[d]runken bouts. Depressive days," and on the day before the divorce, Duniya has "walked in on him pouring out tots of whisky for himself and little Mataan, then eight years old," (29). Taariq is a father that nurtures alcoholism in minors instead of protecting them from it. It is the mother, Duniya that strongly protects the children by throwing Taariq out.

In spite of all Duniya's determination to raise the children Taariq is unable to, men such as her half-brother, Shiriye, believes that a single woman cannot be trusted with parenting. Aside from describing her in a letter as a prostitute, Shiriye, he tells her, "[a] woman needs a man by her side, for people to take her seriously and for the world's doors to open so that she may enter with her head raised and her person respected," (83). Whereas a drunken single male such as Taariq is still respected in the society, a sober single woman such as Duniya is assigned odd names such as "street walker" (82) by the patriarchal society. In the same way, Taariq's brother, Qaasim sexually abuses girls to sire dozens of unwanted children (110).

As a consequence, women's psyches are severely wrecked and exhibit schizophrenic symptoms. Zubair's wife runs mad. As soon as her husband starts pursuing a virgin, she walks to the bushes "builts a fire and began to prepare a meal. While doing this, the woman and her jinni lover were preparing to make love," (36). The concept of the jinn reiterates Islamic concept of majinoon or insanity. Ahmed Okasha and Tare Okasha (2012) observe that *Majnoon,* the Arabic equivalent of "mad," has both positive and negative connotations (74). It refers to shelter, paradise, embryo, shield and madness. The scholars contend that in Islam, a "jinni" is a supernatural spirit lower than angels that can be good or bad. "It is not necessarily a demon or evil spirit," (74b) which is why the young men who follow Zubair's wife do not mistreat her as is the case in Augustan Period where mad people were persecuted (10). When Zubair question her after the death of his virgin, "[s]he entered into a whispered debate with invisible parties. She chuckles" (37) and warns him against blaming his jinn lover. Benard Hart refers to such experiences as hallucinations, defined as false sense impressions or sensory experiences in the absence of any stimulation from the environment (48). C.S Mellor observes that some patients with schizophrenia report having their own thoughts spoken by another voice (16). The remarks made either criticize or encourage the patient; they generally refer to intimate topics related to the patient. Csernansky singles out hallucinations as a symptom of acute schizophrenia (psychosis) (32), since they are a distortion of reality. Zubair's wife dies a few days later.

Furthermore, Duniya experiences psychological disturbances as a result of male domination. Men dominate her life so much that when her brother arrives from abroad, "blood pounded in her ears...*she* couldn't trust her feet to carry her anywhere and her ears were filled with compressed air [...]. *She* was an uncle meeting his nieces and nephews in person for the first time; *she* was a brother meeting his sister Duniya after so many years; she was a man encountering his brother-in-law elect[...]; *she* was a man meeting two good-looking teenagers," (233). This is a hallucinatory experience in which Duniya's self is supplanted by that of men; she sees herself as an uncle, a brother and a man. Her elder brother, Abshir has dominated Duniya's life such that she is absolutely suffocated. He is described as "omnipresent, benevolent," whose shadow "fell on every ramshackle of a structure she built...informing every step she made," (173). As a result, Duniya has lost her female self and her struggle to elevate is vain and fruitless.

Finally, Yussur's father's failure to love her mother results in clinical madness. She sustains a pathological condition, phobia when she eavesdrops her mother saying that she derived more sexual pleasure from suckling Yussur than making love with her father (50). After she bears her first child, Yussur imagines that her mother's experience will be replayed in her life and is beset with dreadful anxiety. "Mire brought a psychiatrist who had a long chat with Yussur, (50), the anxiety subsided, but she locks herself in the bedroom to "feel safe from the mother" (50). In a fit of madness, Yussur throws the baby to the ground to pick a flower. It dies and she kills herself (51). As much as the Yussur's mother seems to be the major cause of insanity, the father is the real culprit. His treatment of her mother resulted in her self-alienation and hence loss of romantic feelings for him.

The plight of women in Farah's *Gifts* is similar to Zakeya and other women characters in Nawal El Saadawi's *God Dies by the Nile*.

Isam Shihada observes that female characters in the novel are "victims of the patriarchal class system consolidated by politics, religions and social customs" (163). Patriarchy is therefore entrenched within the religious and political systems to seal the plight of women, which affects their psyche. Whereas, Shihada proceeds to see "gender oppression as class oppression," this study views gender oppression as a deliberate othering of the female body without association to its material condition.

Zakeya's othering conditions begin while in marriage with her late husband who constantly abused her, physically. The narrator says, "[e]very time a son died, her husband Abdel Moneim struck out at her blindly with anything he would lay hands on," (89). He could beat her whenever he gave birth to a daughter and out of the sixteen children she bore, only one survived- Galal, and the Mayor conscripted her to the army. Besides acts of violence, the act of Moneim siring so many children with Zakeya is meant to limit Zakeya to child bearing.

The cultural setting in Kafr El Teen upholds practices that otherize women and make them vulnerable to insanity. In the character Fatheya Saadawi illuminates the oppressive conditions in which women are compelled to live. As a wife of Sheikh Hamzawi, "her husband was responsible for upholding the teachings of Allah and keeping morals and piety of the village. A wife of a man like that was not supposed to be seen by just anyone. Her body had to be concealed even from her closest relatives except for her face and palms of her hands," (39). Fatheya is therefore forced to make choices about dress contrary to her will. Furthermore, given her marriage to a pious man, her movements around the village are limited. She is expected to live in Sheikh Hamzawi's house "surrounded by all due care and respect never to be seen elsewhere except twice in her life: to be moved from her father's to husband's house; husband's house to the grave," (39). These two movements demonstrate how the destiny of women is limited by patriarchal control. They are enslaved to the man and have to live under their highhanded regime without question. In spite of Hamzawi's impotence and infertility, Fatheya is forced to live under his autocratic control. Her virginity is mechanically broken by Om Saber because of the husband's sexual impairment. The narrator says, "she felt the burning pain left by the woman's finger as it probed up between her thighs looking for blood," (41). Showalter's reference to women as a "cursed" gender is demonstrated when Fatheya is associated with images of uncleanliness in the novel. She is stigmatized to the marginal space:

> Left with something unclean in her body which used to bleed for several days at a time. Each time she had her periods, the people around her would have a changed expression in their eyes when they looked at her or they would avoid her as though there was something corrupt or bad about her," (43).

This excerpt does not just ascertain Showalter's assertion, but reiterates Staszak's argument on stigmatization of basic differences such as sex, ethnicity and race (9). Fatheya's femaleness is branded and she is forced to live with the fragmenting effects of othering. Fatheya in this passage represents all women in Kafr El Teen that experience marginality because of having monthly periods. Men consider them untouchables during their menses, for example Sheikh Hamzawi treats her "as if she was a leper if his hands touched her," (42). He in fact prays to Allah to protect her against the evil Satan (menstruating Fatheya). Whereas other days he would have her listen to Koranic recitations, her husband would not allow her listen to it during her menses.

Ignorance among women is rampant that they remain blind followers of the religion. Of Fatheya, the narrator reports that "she did not understand what the words he [Hamzawi] meant, they were difficult words she kept asking him to explain their meaning," (43).

Although her husband, like all men, understood the words, he gloats in keeping the meanings secret by saying, "[t]he words of Allah and rituals of prayers are supposed to be learnt by heart and not understood," (43). It is a deliberate ploy to keep and maintain religious knowledge as a preserve of men. Perhaps this is why when Zeinab goes to El Sayeda Mosque for healing, she is directed back to The Mayor to sleep with her. The man who is revered as God tells Zeinab "to walk towards the iron gate, open it, walk in and should not walk out again" (115). The Iron Gate represents the Mayors manhood that Zeinab is directed by the patriarchal society to embrace forever.

As a result of gender othering in Zakeya's society, women suffer from diverse strains of mental illness. Zakeya's dreams exhibit high levels of fragmentations that bring back her turbulent marriage. In one of her dreams, "Om Saber (traditional circumciser) leant on her and tried to push her thigh away from the other. Then she pulled out a razor blade from somewhere and proceed to cut her neck," (88). This dream is a reflection of Zakeya's self-alienation, which stems from the traumatizing nature of Female genital mutilation. The circumcisers cutting of her neck signifies the rite's devastating impact on women. El Saadawi suggests that the practice marks the summit of gender othering as it threatens to smother them out of existence. In the same dream, Zakeya sees her husband who "kicks her belly…begins tearing her *galabeya* down her front till her body is exposed" (88) and starts fondling her breasts and thighs. The nightmare signifies the traumatizing marriage experience that left indelible psychological wounds on her. Their sex life was tantamount to rape experience that dealt an irreparable blow to her mental wellbeing.

Zakeya loses her sanity and Om Saber's prayers have little impact on her recovery. During the exorcising of the spirit, she gives a wail, but the problem persists. In Alice Bailey's view, these other selves in pathological persons are as a result of psychic collapse as a creative response to trauma (4). Zakeya's self is supplanted by selves of the persons she hates after the traumatic experiences she undergoes as a result of gender othering.

Zakeya detests the conditions of her life and unless they change, her healing is far from reach. She hates the patriarchal and materialistic leanings of her religion and remonstrates against them. She is therefore alienated from the prayers, which are meant to cure her insanity. Om Saber who prays for her is the very architect of female genital mutilation which maims her sexuality and sheikhs that are said to have healing powers ask for money from the indigent. Disgusted by these cultural elements, she loses interest in prayer. She says, "[m]any a time have I prayed to God...to have mercy on us, but He never seemed to hear me or respond," (89). Zakeya knows, from her past experience that the God of Kafr El Teen is the Mayor and his cabal comprised of male friends. She proceeds to distrust the clerics at El Sayeda Mosque-another clique of men. She tells Hajj Ismail, "[e]ven God wants to pay Him something yet He knows we own nothing," (100). Zakeya in this passage refers to the clique of men who surround the Mayor to bolster patriarchy and perpetuate gender othering of men. Her male opponents are well aware of her agitation and tell her that "her sickness is caused by disobedience" (112). The "disobedience" in this context refers to women's determination to resist the patriarchal domination that turns them into neurotics. On the way to El Sayeda Mosque, Zakeya comes across another woman with mental illness. The husband says, "[s]he refused food and drink, stayed awake all night and got into the habit of talking to herself" (100). Unaware of the oppressive cultural conditions in which his wife lives, the man makes futile visits from sheikh to sheikh until he becomes broke. El Sayeda Mosque is described as a "mighty human ocean" with the "sick or blind, young or old, children or babes..." (112) all of whom are victims of class or gender othering. Having failed to heal Zakeya of her insanity, the sheikhs release her back to the culturally oppressive society. Fed up by the Mayor's perpetuation of gender othering, Zakeya picks a hoe and strikes him dead. Happy to have killed the God who did not hear her prayers, he tells fellow prisoners that she "has killed Allah and is buried on the banks of River Nile," (166). This assertion suggests that Zakeya's insanity stems from the gender and class othering perpetuated by the Mayor and his henchmen and his death portends women's triumph over patriarchal oppression.

Conclusion

From the foregoing discussion, it is apparent that most cases of madness in female characters arise from the oppressive cultural conditions. Women such as Zubair's wife, Duniya, Yussur, Zeinab and Zakeya confront a system that employs state region and politics to keep them at the marginal spaces. Zubair's is so confounded by Zubair's betrayal that she gives up on life in favour of hallucinations that take her mind away. This should be judged in the context of the patriarchal culture that gives men authority to marry as many wives as they can as long as they can pay their way. Similarly, the Culture gives Abdel Monem powers to beat his wife Zakeya any time he feels like it. The violence meted out on her to the extent of damaging her mental health stems from her cultural landscape. The religion seems to have embraced patriarchy so much that Zakeya can no longer pray because any such action is tantamount to the loyalty pledge to the patriarchal institution.

Madness and the Other in Farah's *Close Sesame* and Matar's *The Return*

Madness is any deviation from rational reality of the societal norm; something undesirable.

Gregory Reid

A mad individual is anybody whose behaviour does not conform to the conventions of society.

Michel Foucault

Madness has been construed by some scholars as the state of being different from one's community. By virtue of being deviant, the individual is incorporated among the abnormal hence perceiving otherness as insanity in itself. The other is relegated by the rest of the community because they already are mad. In his phenomenal work, *Madness and Civilisation* Michel Foucault observes that during the Augustan period, the European society imprisoned "poor vagabonds, criminals and the unemployed" (7) because they did not conform to conventions that exhorted people to work hard and acquire material prosperity. Anyone who behaved in a manner that did not conform to the morals of society; anyone who looked miserable was undesirable and confined to the asylum. Gregory Reid reiterates Foucault's argument by associating madness with any behaviour that runs counter to reason. He singles out among others, tendencies towards fantasy, religious beliefs and temper tantrums (15).

While it is understandable to denote add behaviour as insanity, it is inaccurate to neglect the possible causes of such strangeness. To some societies, a young person engrossed in music walking around with earphones is "the other" by reason of their addiction to phantasy. According to Reid and Foucault (in context of Augustan epoch) the phantasy is madness without any attempt to investigate the cause of the young man's otherness. Such a thesis is shallow as it assumes the symptom as madness and absolves possible causes of the behaviour from blame. It is in fact amazing to discover that aspects of otherness (discrimination) could be the actual causes of the young man's phantasy. As much as the obsession sets apart the youth as the other, a more critical examination of their condition may reveal that an aspect of otherness is possibly the cause of the otherness. Donald Roberts notes, "[i]nsanity is more subject to cultural and ideological underpinnings than medical considerations" (10) and any reasonable treatment for insanity should consider the cultural context. Jon Anderson defines culture as what humans do (3) and it encompasses all aspects of society: politics, economy, [my emphasis], religion, education, family and commerce. Any deviance in any of these organs of society will have devastating consequences on the mental life of the people in that society.

Roberts elaborates that Ronald Laing sees in the mad an exaggeration of traits already present in the cultural milieu. Roberts cites Laing, "[t]he patient is the truth, not revealing truth, just the raw edge, the fragmented, dangerous symbol of deep ulcation within human interaction," (13). Roberts asserts that Laing agrees that locating the source of madness within the patient serves to deflect criticism from cultural causes and that madness is often a symbol of corrosive societal influences (13). In other words, referring to the aforementioned music addict as mad is an attempt to absolve the vices in the cultural milieu that are responsible for his or her addiction.

This is the conversation to which Frantz Fanon belongs, and he expounds how the political arm of society can invent *otherness* and drive the subjects to mental illness. In league with Fanon's perspective, Felix Mnthali contends that dictatorship in the family and politics constitute Farah's vision in *Close Sesame*. The unnamed General introduces an oppressive system that affects everyone in Somalia. Unfortunately, no one is able to dislodge him from the "strangle hold which he exercises on his country" (53). Mnthali expounds that the General is only concerned about three clans: The Marehan (his clan), the Ogaden (his mother's clan) and the Dulbahante, his son in law's clan (53). The divide and rule along clan lines is combined with marginalization of the intelligentsia to prolong his autocratic rule. He expedites this through "cooptation and ethnic rivalries to mobilize the population against particular groups" (60). Mnthali's study expounds on otherness, which is a concept of investigation in this study. The General adopts ethnic otherness in his rule, which results in psychological anomalies in Deeriye and Khaliif. This study will focus on political and racial otherness in the selected texts and interrogate their effects on the mental health of characters.

Literary scholars have also demonstrated how trauma resulting from dictatorial regimes haunts characters and adversely affects their mental health. Claudia Kramatschek observes that in Matar's *The Return*, the writer shows a son's traumatic experience after the disappearance of his loving father. Kramatschek adds that Hisham confronts the ghost of his past, which is the father's disappearance and the "shattered dream of a new Libya that his father would have brought to realization" (para 1). Kramatschek's ideas are invaluable to this study as they show the effect of political otherness on the self of the characters. The "son's traumatic experience" is indirect reference to the fragmented self in relation to Hisham, which is a reference to Fanon's "psychic collapse," in this study. Similarly, Rachel Cooke asserts that *The Return* is not a story about Qaddafi's autocratic regime, but a novel about "family and loss," (para, 5). Cooke adds that Matar writes of the paralyzing anger he felt as a young man when he had to leave Libya against his will, then his father was kidnapped. She writes, "[i]t is in his turning away that we feel his unfathomable sorrow," (para, 9). In the novel, Matar is embittered by exile rather than Qaddafi's cruelty. Cooke's review suggests that otherness arises from diasporic dislocation and may result in psychic collapse.

This chapter extends the thesis that otherness is a systematized negation of the other that results in madness. Using the postcolonial theory, the chapter overturns the flippant treatment of madness as otherness using new evidence from Farah's *Close Sesame* and Matar's *The Return*.

3.3 Political Otherness and Psychopathy in *Close Sesame* and *The Return*

Political otherness refers to stigmatization of characters based on their political beliefs or nationality. In this subsection, political otherness will be used synonymously with ideological otherness given the thin line that exists between ideology and positions held by different people politically in our world today. Martin Antony defines ideology as an orientation of political parties or beliefs that are relevant to a political party (9). Theodore Adorn, Brunswk Frenkel Levinson Daniel and Sanford Nevitt define ideology as a set of beliefs, attitudes and values (2). They therefore widen the scope to encompass religious and cultural values of a society. However, this subsection adopts Anthony Down's definition of ideology as "verbal image of the good society and the chief means of constructing such a society" (96). The "good society" to some will be realized by dictatorship and to others by democracy. The "ideal society" to one will be realized by conservatism and to another by liberalism.

Political or ideological otherness in Farah's *Close Sesame* and Matar's *The Return* takes the trajectory of Fanon's otherness and the colonial subject. The French's systematic negation of the Africans in Algeria (182) and the frenzied attempt to deny them all attributes of humanity, which for a while is left unchallenged leading to psychic collapse and madness is a replica of the Somali and Libya experience in the texts. Political otherness in the two novels from ideological differences between those who believe in dictatorship and those who uphold democracy and Islam as means to Downs' "good society" in Libya and Somalia. Hisham's father, in Matar's *The Return* leads a camp of dissidents who disapprove Muamar Gaddafi's style of leadership. The dictator stigmatizes Jaballa and his supporters via a series of repressive acts. Hisham and his father, Jaballa flee Libya in 1979 and settle in Cairo in 1980. This is the beginning of the family's exile. Hisham writes, "Rome, a vacation spot for us; London, where I went at the age of fifteen [...]" (3). Since his rise to power in 1969 through a military coup, Gaddafi shows intolerance towards those who cherish democracy as a means to an ideal society. Matar writes:

> In any political history of Libya, the 1980s represent a particularly lurid chapter. Opponents of the regime were hanged in public and sports arenas. Dissidents who fled the country were pursued- some kidnapped or assassinated. The eighties were also the first time that Libya had an armed resistance to the dictatorship. (4)

This text depicts the regime's distaste for the ideological other through the inhumane treatment of the opposition supporters. They are arrested and hanged in public as warning to any Libyans who might be tempted to oppose Gaddafi's ideology. In the same way, post-independence Somali governments perpetuate Italian totalitarianism and highhandedness that are at variant to Deeriye's ideology of humility and service to the people in Farah *Close Sesame*. A general overthrows the government and like Jaballa Matar in *The Return*, Deeriye and his family disapprove his style of leadership. Paul Zeleza observes, "[i]n Farah's Trilogy, the ruthless General is not an arbitrary superficial presence...but an embodiment of the articulation between traditional despotism and modern state terror," (18). Zeleza suggests that the General's dictatorship is terribly severe because it is entrenched in the traditional "patriarchal family" and clan system. Stipended chiefs like Haj Omer and Cigaal support the dictatorship thereby dividing the Somali community ideologically. There is Deeriye, his son Mursal, Mahad, Mukhtaar, Ahmed, Jibril, Koschin, Medina, Samater,

Sicilian and Willie, (222) on one hand and Cigaal, Sheikh Ibrahim, Yassin, Haj Omer's son and the General on the other hand. Mukhtaar is Sheikh Ibrahim's son who differs with his father and takes Mursal's and Mahad's ideology. Cigaal is Deeriye's neighbour, described as, "[a] collaborator of Italians, a betrayer of friends, some of whom were said to have died under torture later," (75), hails from the General's clan and thereby supports the regime. Mahad is the son of the man who killed the Italian soldier in 1934 and he continues with his father's resistance against political oppression (36). With Mursal, they lead an underground revolutionary movement against the General's dictatorship.

Whereas Cigaal and Sheikh Ibrahim support the dictator, Deeriye has an organic spite for dictatorship. Felix Mnthali observes that dictatorship in the family and state and the individual's search for identity constitutes Farah's vision in *Close Sesame* (53). Indeed Deeriye wonders why the General renames Somalia as Somalia Democratic Republic and renders the "democratic" portion of the name a mere decoration, "an embellishment of the worst kind" (100-101). The General makes a mockery of the democratic ideology during elections by painting one ballot box with colours of the national flag and then label the other box, "only the enemy of the nation need use this," (101). In a soliloquy, Farah brings to the fore Deeriye's spite for authoritarian system of leadership:

> Keep the populace underinformed so you can rule them; keep them apart by informing them separately; build bars of ignorance around them, imprison them with shackles of uninformedness [sic] and they are easy to govern; feed them with wrong information, give them poisonous bits of what does not count, a piece of gossip here, a rumour there, an unconfirmed report. (82)

Mnthali expounds that in his oppressive tactics over the people in *Close Sesame*, the General has joined the conventional African dictators that no one is able to dislodge from power (53). Like Jaballa Matar in *The Return*, Deeriye's contemptuous attitude towards political autocracy in *Close Sesame* is amazing inspiration to the young generation as embodied in his son, Mursal and Mahad. Although his dilapidated state of health cannot allow him to take the front line in leading a revolution, his son and Mahad champion it. In a conversation with Mursal and Mahad, Deeriye talks about the Islamic tradition and thought, the constitution of Medina, (85) to possibly prove that the General has negated them. They discuss the law of retaliation to probably find a revolutionary solution to the regime's oppression. In a dialogue with his friend, Rooble, he reveals that Mursal, Mahad and Mukhtaar run an underground organization that plans to overthrow the dictatorship and replace it with a democratic government (107). Deeriye stumbles on three revolvers under Mahad's mattress.

Furthermore, the Gaddafi regime in *The Return* forbids Jaballa's family from travelling outside the country to punish them for Jaballa's opposition to the regime (77). In court, Uncle Mohamoud and other members of the opposition are not allowed to hire defense lawyers and are all charged with treason (83). The regime's othering tactics are extended to the media. There is no media freedom particularly for members of the opposition. Ahmed Al-Faitouri, an editor of Al-Haqiqah newspaper tells Hisham that Libyan journalism is a "battered institution" (113) because journalists are censored, imprisoned and even killed. He adds that the regime's repeated assaults on bookshops- confiscating their stock and closing some of them down made it almost impossible to find books in Libya thereby achieving their aim of keeping the masses ignorant. (116). The regime's discrimination against writers is evident not only in banning of Hisham's books in Libya but through arrest and incarceration of Ahmed and other writers in a fake book festival (117). In *Close Sesame*, Deeriye's family and clan are a marked one because of their history of resistance and the media can only be used to taint them negatively. Deeriye has borne everything patiently: the relegation of his family in political appointments, the public humiliations for refusing to support the General; it is the realization that his son Mursal is possibly assassinated that is terribly unbearable. Although he had not been there to bring him up, Deeriye loved Mursal who at present was looking after him. Deeriye and twelve elders of the clan are rounded up after refusing to surrender the young man who had killed the Italian soldier and detained. This isolates him from his new wife, Nadiifa. His social life goes to shambles as he spends many years alone in prison.

Deeriye can only meet his wife in the mind. He thinks:

> Love came later in detention, when she (Nadiifa) visited him in his visionary dreams; love came much later when both passed the test of endurance; a woman who was also a friend; to make all this richer, he had friends with whom he had grown up and of whom he was very fond. (35)

The squalid and lonely conditions of prison life had debilitated Deeriye to the current conditions of senile dementia. Similarly, the prisoners and their relatives in Matar's *The Return* are maltreated by reason of their political ideology. The authorities have supplied prisoners' with family books listing all the members of the nuclear family. The agents of the regime check update and return the books. One family discovers a change many years later when they take the book to register a newborn. They are confounded to realize that their imprisoned grandfather "had been dead for several years" (248). One woman who has always thought the record in the book is fine wakes up at night and when she flips through the family book is stunned to see a "line written in strong blue ink against her son's name, 'died in 1996 of natural causes". (249). The woman is heard screaming "years" and people cannot tell whether she means the years she would endure without her son or the five years she wasted visiting her son with cooked meals, gifts and writing letters for a dead son. Apparently, the prison wardens have been throwing away letters, eating the food and selling the gifts meant for such prisoners just because they are "the political other". Although Deeriye in *Close Sesame* manages to leave prison, his only son, raised by his brother in law is assassinated.

He cannot in his fragmented state, live without Mursal. In a stream consciousness, he asks, "[w]hat if it were somebody else trying to communicate the news that Mursal had died? Yes, what if he were dead?" (224). Such a possibility would bring Deeriye to the final precipice of political otherness. The possibility was quite certain given the General's determination to crush the underground movement. Zeinab tells Deeriye the General's assertions:

> It is not the heads of cattle but people that will be rolling this time- the General's appears to imply. And the General means business. No unnatural droughts to be created, for the natural famine claims lives daily and a nationalist war in Ogaden. (181)

Deeriye and his group of insurgents (members of his family and clan) should prepare for arrests; grilling, torture and detention given that people close to him such as Mahad have made an attempt on his life. The government controlled radio articulately announces Mahad's failure to kill the General to facilitate the revolutionaries' relegation. Deeriye cannot take the news of

Mursal's disappearance for granted. Although he has been invited to talk to the General, he is aware of his political otherness. The host of this invitation is his sworn enemy- an autocratic military ruler who violates the tenets of Deeriye's religion to mismanage the affairs of the nation; an evil ruler who uses financial resources of the nation to install sycophantic chiefs from his clan to oppress the masses. John Hawley suggests that General's absence in the novel is an attempt to make himself a god around which the people's lives are defined (192). This is inconsistent to the religion Deeriye professes and he resolves, like Mahad before him, to go alone and kill the General: "[t]hen with a service revolver hidden, go, meet the General: and kill. What? "Yes, kill,' said a voice inside him." The voice persuades him that he is not killing to vindicate himself, but for the sake of justice for all Somalians that have suffered under the totalitarian regime. Mnthali sums up Deeriye's failure to kill the General as the consequence their political marginalization, which Fiona Moolla specifies as fragmentation arising from isolation from society (57).

The pinnacle of political otherness in Matar's *The Return* is reached when prisoners complain of mistreatment and are herded into an open yard and massacred. In a painful reminiscence, Hmad, one of Hisham's uncles narrates the tragic events of that day. The prisoners protest that they do not have even animal rights (266) and Sennussi, Qaddafi's henchman rants, "[w]e are government and you are prisoners. If we want, we can tonight send fighter jets to bomb the entire prison with you and the guards in it," (266). The opposition from Adjdabiya- Hisham's father's village- are asked to identify themselves: Ali, Mohamoud and Ahmed do so, but Hisham's father does not. They are separated and the rest (including Hisham's father) are taken to an open yard. Hmad narrates:

A few seconds later, we heard a loud explosion, then dense and unceasing gunfire- all sorts of weapons, machine guns and the sound of men screaming all coming from the workshop...it turned out that Abdullah Sennussi had initiated the massacre by throwing a hand grenade into the workshop. The shooting lasted for two hours. (269)

This is the apex of political otherness at Abu Salim Prison in which 1, 270 prisoners, including Jaballa Matar were massacred. Their bodies were buried where they fell in shallow mass graves. To demonstrate the regime's hate for the political other, the bodies are exhumed, ground to dust and powder and poured into the sea (270). The message hits Hisham with incredible pain as it confirms the futility of his efforts to find his father, Jaballa Matar. Similarly the worse case of political otherness in *Close Sesame* is witnessed in 1934 during the Italian incursion of Deeriye's clan when the new Italian administrator orders him to hand over a young man who has sought asylum in his village. The Italian administrator try to compel a neighbouring Sultan to appoint stipended chiefs that will be answerable to the Italian but he declines (35). The Italians try to force their way into the Sultan's houses and a Somali young man wrestles with the Italian soldier to usurp the gun in his grip. A stray bullet is released during the hustle and hits the Italian soldier who dies within thirty minutes. The young man seeks asylum in Deeriye's village, but Haj Omer informs the Italians where he is. The Italian administrator arrives at Deeriye's to demand for the young man and Deeriye declines.

The insolence and arrogance typical of otherness are quite evident throughout the episode. First, the territory in question is Somali land and we expect the Italian foreigner to approach the Sultan with decorum and request for a place to lease or lodge. The decision to force their way into the Sultan's house is a terrible act of otherness. To the Italians, there are no people in that house (Somalis are not people), but "the natural environment" in Fanon's opinion. They are taken aback when the young man wrestles the soldier and kills him. The Italian administrator, while asking for the young man who killed the Italian, does it arrogantly. It is grilling rather than enquiry. The narrator says that he uses "yes or no questions" and Deeriye is not given room to explain. The Italian is the "self" and Deeriye the "other" to be treated like a misbehaved child before a responsible father. Following this, the Italians send a punitive expedition to Deeriye's community; they poison the wells and using bazookas, shoot cattle to cripple it economically. The narrator writes:

> An evening later, Deeriye heard a pandemonium of shouts and cries. Before this died down, there came voices of appeal; then the painful moaning of cattle struggling with departing life. This made sense when he heard shots, then the thud of a target struck, a target of heads of cattle. (41)

Given that Deeriye has not co-ordinated with other Somali clans to resist the incursion, he feels lonely and hopeless. Moreover, the Italian colonial administration in *Close Sesame* rewards Somali collaborators by paying them monthly allowances and segregates those who resist its policies. There is therefore an ideological difference based on resistance and collaboration, which enhances political otherness in the Somali society. Deeriye's clansman, Haj Omer supports the Italians right from their first appearance in Somali land. He betrays the clan by informing on the young man who kills the Italian and the clan suffers the painful consequences. The colonialists reward him; he is crowned a stipended chief, which sows stigma between his followers and Deeriye's. The narrator says, "Haj Omer was a traitor, resolved to excommunicate him, but the Italians and subsequent national governments kept him on the payroll," (183). During the clan meeting, Waris drives his son away for their history of collaboration and betrayal. In Matar's The *Return*, there are many characters such as Haj Omer and collaborators. Qaddafi pays them to hunt and kill revolutionaries in all parts of the world. Revolutionaries that flee to foreign countries like Jaballa Matar, Hisham's father are not safe. They live in constant fear of being arrested and killed. As a consequence, a renowned Libyan economist who was stepping off a train at Stazione Termini in Rome is assassinated by Gaddafi's spy. The man "[p]ressed a pistol on his chest and pulled a trigger," (5). A Libyan student is sitting on a terrace of a café in Monastiraki Square in Greece when he is shot dead (5-6) and a Libyan British Broadcasting Service Newsreader is killed in London (6). Hisham's brother Ziad terminates his studies in Switzerland and returns to Cairo in fear of Libyan spies

Clans and families in *Close Sesame* experience ideological differences that result in otherness and consequent insanity. One glaring example is the story of Mukhtaar, Sheikh Ibrahim's son.

Unlike his father who subscribes to the dictatorial style of leadership, Mukhtaar detests it and joins Mursal and Mahad to plan how to dethrone the system. Sheikh Ibrahim is so embittered by Mukhtaar's decision and swears to kill him. Rooble tells Deeriye that the major disagreement between Mukhtaar and his father have to do with ideological differences," (48). Mukhtaar believes in the nationalist course and therefore finds the dictatorial, military regime a liability to the citizens. Consequently, he breaks ranks with his father to sabotage the system, which costs him his sanity and life. On the contrary, families in Matar's *The Return* choose ideological leanings and stand by them. Hisham Matar's family has had a long history of resistance descending from Grandfather Hamed who joined armed resistance to fight against Italian incursion in Libya.

His son Jaballa resisted Qadafi's autocratic regime and paid the ultimate prize for freedom: his own life. When Seif, Qaddafi's son Seif calls Hisham and suggests that they should be good friends. Hisham answers the call, but uses a tone that is not his at the time. He replies, "[p]eople can't choose their history," but says, "hearing that cold mechanical tone return," (208). The "cold mechanical tone" is possibly his father's self that emerges to respond to the family's arch- enemy as reminder that Qaddafi's family cannot work in a binary opposition with Jaballa's.

Finally, ideological otherness in Matar's *The Return* and Farah's *Close Sesame* is also evident in Jaballa's and Deeriye's attitude towards the love of money that comes with the introduction of cash economy during colonialism. The two revolutionaries cherish religious values more than material things, which probably affect their sanity. When he returns from prison, most of his Deeriye's colleagues have changed from passion for moral and religious ideals to adoration of money and property. His stubborn insistence on idealism sets him apart as ideologically different and alienates him. In a stream consciousness, he says:

> They deliberately do not wish to have any dealings with ideas and national principles they believe they are of no immediate concern to them, only whether or not the clan they are spoken of is getting the share the government has promised (it doesn't matter whether the government is national or colonial, democratic or fascist): nothing matters so long as they are made content); they make do with scrapings and breadcrumbs or worse, hand-me-down gifts from anyone. (107-108)

In this text, Deeriye expresses his contempt for new culture in which people are absolutely

disinterested in knowledge and wisdom and swapped it for what can enable them survive: money. They therefore become easy prey to deceptive leaders who bribe them and continue mismanaging the nation. This realization infuriates Deeriye and alienates him from them. This could be the major reason why he does not visit them. In an internal monologue, he says, "[f]riendship is a very complicated organizational concept of self and group definition; and I would define myself out of this lot; any day," (108). He says this of Afrah and Daahir's friendship because they only value him by how much he is worth. Concerning his son's (Mursal) marriage to the American wife, they only look at "how much money the wife must have brought" (108). Deeriye holds this materialistic thinking in contempt and isolates himself all the time. Similarly, Jaballa's hate for materialism in Matar's *The Return* is demonstrated by his generosity. Unlike Qaddafi who enriches himself by buying properties in Europe (140), Jaballa spends his money on the beggars in his home town. Hisham says that Jaballa would join labourers and street sweepers, sit on the ground in his fine clothes, share their meal and then "slide bank notes beneath the plate," (66). He insists that his children should never deny any needy person anything. When they get hint of his presence, they queue in his compound and when Hisham complains of fraud, Jaballa tells him, "[i]t is not your job to read their hearts," (66). Jaballa's is a singular philosophy that crowns him the other in a greedy and materialistic world.

As a consequence of political otherness, characters in Matar's *The Return* and Farah's *Close Sesame* suffer from diverse strains of madness. In Hisham's neighbourhood, before he leaves with his father to exile, many people run mad because of the oppressive political circumstances.

He writes:
> One of the ways that my parents tried to shield Ziad and me from the madness that was unraveling outside our home was by making sure that every minute of our day was filled. We went to school, returned just in time for piano lessons, had lunch, then were off to El Medina el Sahiya Club for swimming. We would spend the rest of the day by the sea; the sea was our territory. There were a few adults around, but they were so eccentric that they seemed part of our imagination. (36)

Qaddafi's purge and inhumane treatment of critics such as hanging of university students in public squares devastates the people's psyches and Jaballa Matar is compelled to protect his children from such consequences.

Hisham gives more examples of people who underwent psychic collapse as the aftermath of the oppression. There is an old man, with milky eyes who sat all day by the harbor, fishing, but no one ever saw him catch anything (37). This is similar to aimless idling typical of catatonic schizophrenia. There is El-Hindi, a Native American who had ended up in Tripoli after killing a white American and fleeing. He would stand on the bridge by the harbor and dive with his arms outstretched, bringing them together only before entering the water (37). Although El-Hindi likes to show off his swimming skills, he is quite unstable mentally. Whereas political otherness in *The Return* results in clinical madness, in *Close Sesame* it drives Deeriye and Khaliif to religious insanity or fanaticism. Deeriye and Khaliif exhibit this in their attempt to confront a dictatorial regime that exploits ethnicity to perpetuate its misrule. Deeriye is deeply engrossed in the worship of Allah that he has no time for anything else. His world and all its experiences are interpreted in accordance with the Holy Quran. Moolla expounds on Deeriye's piety as a person that "seems to exist at different levels of consciousness at once. The narrative (*Close Sesame*) presents him passing seamlessly from waking to sleep, from reality to dream world which prophetically foreshadows future events outside of the procedurally rational order" (183). Moolla suggests that unlike other characters such as Mursal that live by the natural conscious level that thinks to make decisions, Deeriye is guided by other marginal levels of consciousness that are irrational to the rational world. Moolla singles out his communication with the spirit of his late wife Nadiifa as a "prophetic experience" (183) similar to that of the founder of Islam.

Deeriye's obsession with religion brings to the fore the controversial interaction between religion and the material world that has sometimes resulted in conflicts between the laity and those who do not believe in religion. The emergence of Rationality during the Enlightment period underscored the separation of reason from the irrational and madness and religion were categorized as irrational (Caputo, 25). The preoccupation of religion with abstract unconscious processes and the proclamation of the unseen deity are inconsistent with concerns of reason in a material world. Lillian Feder sees this preoccupation of unconscious processes over conscious ones as madness (5). Such people rely on visions, dreams, and oracles rather than reason to go about their lives in the world. Caputo writes:

> In pre-modern times, we said God is truth. In modernity, we separate religion from truth and redescribe it as a protected right...in modernity, religion is a matter of private conscience; it is formally a protected right even if it is materially a bit mad. (28)

Caputo in the above assertion consigns religion to the sphere of madness possibly because of its concern with abstract things. Jacques Derrida, an indomitable voice of Enlightment, describes St Augustine's religious books and prayers as mere parody and "irrelevant bit of impudence from an avant-garde writer". He adds that Augustine's works are irrational and "perhaps even mad" (15) and therefore not deserving an honorary degree from Cambridge. This is how these proponents of rationality will describe characters such as Deeriye and Khaliif.

Political otherness in Matar's *The Return* results in many other odd mental symptoms. When Matar goes to Abu Salim Prison when prisoners are being released, there is a man whose mind reacts to situations illogically. Matar says that the man could stop breathing and faint whenever he heard news that made him laugh or cry (84) and the only solution was to slap him hard on the back. Hisham introduces a teenager to him and asks him what his name is. When the teenager identifies himself, the man faints and no amount of beating on the back makes him come to. The boy is possibly his son because the man has been in prison for a long time and we expect him to rejoice, but he completely loses consciousness. The reaction is symptomatic of severe or illogical thought disturbance. The regime detains the man with the strange sickness for over a decade because of his divergent political ideology, which is political otherness. The detention has had debilitating effect on his cognitive powers. Similarly, political otherness in *Close Sesame* leads to extremities in religious practices. When *Close Sesame* begins, Deeriye prays:

> He moved in the direction of the lavatory, which was on the same floor. He said *Acuudubilaahi* as he entered the toilet which he thought of as Satan's dwelling place, and when he came out, having taken his ablution, said *Alxamdulillaah*. Then another prayer, this time of only two prostrations- the morning's *salaatus subx*! The beads again. A litany of Koranic verses. As he counted and recounted the ninety nine names of Allah, as he multiplied and subtracted

the number of times he had said them, he realized that the world had begun to wake up. (4)

To the modernist, Deeriye's actions in this passage are irrational because the toilet, which is a waste disposal area, is for Deeriye Satan's home and a special prayer has to be made before entering. Since it is unclean a place, he has to take ablution to cleanse himself before praying. The prostration to the modernist is dabbling comedy because the deity being worshipped is unseen and so the praises he is given by the counting of beads and names is sheer insanity. In the ensuing text, Deeriye vows not to think of his neighbours, betrayals and conspiracies, his good friends, Rooble and Elmi Tiir, but focus on "God; of prayers and his divine will" (4). As much as rationality does not incorporate such religious practices, Socrates associates many positive results with religious dedication (Lindstrom, 56).

In his work *Phaedrus*, Socrates asserts that madness which comes from the gods is superior to sanity, which is of human origin. He singles out four categories of madness: prophecy, which is given the Greek name *mantiken epipnoian* that is inspired by Apollo; mystic madness from the Greek word *telestiken* inspired by Dionysus, the poetic from the Greek word *poientiken*, inspired by Muses and the madness of love *Erotiken manian* inspired by Aphrodite and Eros (Lindstrom, 57-58). Socrates concludes that the greatest blessings come to us through madness, which is sent as a gift from the gods. Socrates' assertions are evident in the life of Deeriye in *Close Sesame* and Jaballa in *The Return*. Their dedication to Allah has resulted in many positive results: they are famous and respected for their courage against colonialism and dictatorship. Their children are successful, Mursal, a lecturer, Zeinab a medical doctor and Hisham Matar is an author of international repute. Deeriye can afford to brag in his old age:

> I can afford to hold to my principles and keep them: I am wealthy; my son is well placed and is married to an American: my daughter is a medical doctor. They give thought not to a pressing nationalist questions but to whether or not one can afford this or that principle. The acoustics, which echo their fears...their hopes and the positions they take: materialism. (107)

Given his economic independence, Deeriye can oppose the regime because he does not have to depend on the General's stipends. Zeinab draws parallels between his biography and those of legends of human history (142). After the invasion of his land and the ensuing massacre of livestock, many saw his defiance as madness. For Socrates, nothing hurts a good man and so was Deeriye's courageous stance towards the invaders. Deeriye's name is a cause of anxiety to the regime because he inspires resistance and courage against oppression; in a mad kamikaze act like that employed by Mahad, Deeriye arrives at the General's award giving ceremony and instead of pulling out the revolver, takes out prayer beads to shoot the General. Summing up the story, the narrator asserts, "[h]e was an easy target now that he had not hit his. And the General's bodyguards emptied into him cartridges of machine-gun fire until his body was cut nearly in half," (260). Besides allotting him mental illness, political otherness brings Deeriye to a catastrophic end in Farah's *Close Sesame*. Hawley concludes that although religion is ineffective in dislodging political otherness, it is "powerful in providing one's vision of oneself" (192) and hope in misery. Hawley expounds that in death "Deeriye embodies...Islamic devotion" (195) which Farah views as the true weapon that will dislodge the dictatorship.

One interesting thing in Matar's *The Return* and Farah's *Close Sesame* is how some members of the dominant group exhibit symptoms of madness. Although he belongs to the dominant group, Seif, Qaddafi's son, exhibits symptoms of cognitive dysfunction. He makes a speech after the commencement of the revolution and Matar describes it as follows:

> The long pauses between his repeated statements were so extended… in different ways, he repeated the same claim: Libyans abroad were conspiring against the country. Everything he said was repeated countless times. The contents of his speech which lasted thirty eight minutes could have been communicated in three minutes. (234)

Matar suggests that Seif's psyche is so deranged that he cannot give an elaborate logical speech about the situation affecting the country. The subject of the speech is that Libyans abroad conspire against the state, which a sane speaker can deliver in three minutes, but he takes long, which exhibits the schizophrenic's repetitions in speech making. Similarly, Farah suggests that the General in *Close Sesame* is mad. He cannot even trust those who work for him. He visits a mental hospital and enjoys talking to the audience of the insane. There is a man who refuses to laugh or smile at his speech and when the General asks who the mad man is, the director replies that the man is the only man in "the room" who was declared sane that morning (20).

The General feigns happiness then irritably growls, "[y]ou are mad yourself…straitjacket him, quick…" (20). The director is detained for stating facts that morning. Given that the two writers link otherness to psychic collapse, could this imply that dictators are possible victims of otherness during childhood?

3.4 Racial Otherness and Pathology in *The Return* and *Close Sesame*

Racial otherness and its psychological consequences on their characters are evident in selected texts. In *The Return*, there are few instances of racial otherness. In this autobiography, it manifests through Italian pacification and occupation of Libya. Fanon in *The Wretched of the Earth* asserts that there is a nexus between colonialism and racism. He writes:

> What parcels out the world is the fact of belonging to a race... in the colonies; the economic substructure is also a superstructure. The cause is the consequence: you are rich because you are white; you are white because you are rich. The governing race, first and foremost, are those who come from elsewhere, those who are like the original inhabitants, "the others." (40)

Fanon here emphasizes both racial and economic othering of the colonized peoples during colonialism. The leaders of the system had to be white especially in French and Portuguese colonies where direct rule (assimilation) was employed. The "others" in this text refers to the whites; Fanon suggests that otherness also applies to the oppressor because he or she gloats in a narcissistic kind of self-importance.

Bloated in the myth of racial superiority, the Italians invade Libya in 1911 and start occupying its cities as if they have no human inhabitants. Matar's grandfather, Hamed, joins the resistance against Italian invaders (150). Matar gives the background to the Libyan revolt (1911-1916) during which five thousand Libyans are banished from the city and sent to small islands scattered around

Italy. Given that Tripoli had a population of about 30,000 people, then one in every six inhabitants of the city was kidnapped and made to disappear, (152) . The five thousand comprise of the most distinguished of Libyans: wealthy traders, scholars, jurists and bureaucrats; Matar concludes that this act of otherness "was an extraordinary example of a European occupying power devastating a city," (153). The cruelty of this punitive expedition possibly stems from the Italian's disappointment. When they set off from Italy, they do not expect to find any honourable person in Africa, but are shocked to find scholars, wealthy traders and other noble persons. It pricked the racist delusion that Africa is a dark continent to be civilized via colonialism. Similarly, racial otherness in Farah's *Close Sesame* is depicted through crude Italian invasion of Deeriye's community without the slightest recognition of his administration as a Sultan. Expounding on Fanon's sentiments on racism and colonialism, Satre asserts that the colonizer believes "[o]n the other side of the ocean there is a race of less than humans, who thanks to us, might reach our status a thousand years hence," (26). Satre suggests that colonialists saw Africans as sub-humans who could only improve their status by their help. This is evident when Deeriye rejects Italian's order to surrender the young man who had killed the Italian soldier; they want to force their way into one of Deeriye's houses (35). The Italians do not see a leader of human persons in Deeriye, but a mere animal such as donkey to be shoved about. In an omniscient narration, Farah links the colonial enterprise to racial otherness:

> History was a string of intolerable nonsense of dominations that were called civilising missions; of "pacifying" expeditionary forces which looted and raped and robbed while they misdescribed those "masskillings" as the ennobblement of the savage: turned countries into colonies, the colonies into peaceful commercial centres;

> pacify 30,000 population of indigenous extraction so that the 300 Italians could live as Masters[...]. (104)

This passage echoes Levi Strauss assertion that humankind's failure to accommodate basic differences like culture and race leads to the description of the other as "savage" (11), hence the need for pacification. In this text, Italian invasion of Somalia had little to do with civilising the Somalis; Farah suggests that it was expression of Italian racial superiority over the Somali community. The specified numbers attest to the Italian superiority since one Italian is equal to a hundred Somalis in value.

In the same way, Matar traces the Libyan resistance against colonialism and the inhuman treatment of the leaders of the resistance movement. Just like Kenya where racial hatred played out in the callous assassination of resistance leaders such as Koitalel Arap Samoei, Omar al- Mukhtaar, the leader of the Libyan revolt is arrested and after a show trial, hanged on the outskirts of Benghazi (157). The Italian colonial administrators ensure that Omar al-Mukhtaar's execution is attended by a large number of Libyans. The racial otherness is evident during the Italian campaign to crash the revolt. Matar writes:

> After the Fascists marched on Rome in 1922 and Benito Mussolini seized power, the destruction and slaughter took on a massive scale. Air power was employed to gas and bomb villages. The policy was that of depopulation. History remembers Mussolini as the buffoonish Fascist, the ineffective silly man who led a lame military campaign in the Second World War but in Libya, he oversaw a campaign of genocide. (153)

This passage proves Fanons' assertion about the othered colonial subject. The Italians consider the Libyans as the natural environment thereby using airpower to gas and bomb villages as if not a single person lives there. The mention of Mussolini echoes our introductory remarks about Adolf Hitler, the German dictator during the Second World War. Hitler and Mussolini shared racist and Fascist maxims that brought them together in the Anti-comintern Pact of 1936 (Walsh, 262), to isolate Russia due to her race and ideology.

As a consequence of racial otherness, Muftah in Matar's *The Return* has brain dysfunction by reason of his odd behaviour in the novel. In a dialogue between Hisham and Uncle Mahmoud, the reader learns that Muftah is Jaballa's cousin and therefore Hisham's kin. When Hisham arrives at his uncle's home, he is shocked at how Muftah keeps repeating his greetings. Hisham says that Muftah keeps saying, "[a]re you well? Your health? Your family?" (73). Hisham attempts to reply thoroughly but is disappointed to realize that Muftah is not interested in the answers Hisham gives him. He says Muftah's "questions continued and seemed more ridiculous yet also poignant with each repetition" (73). Worse still, his mind has broken down such that he does not like the company of people. His son says, "[h]e goes to be with his camels, he loves them more than his own family," (72). Muftah's mind cannot enable him to live with people; it has so disintegrated that he lives with camels. Gerald Davison refers to Muftah's condition as schizophrenia, a mental disorder characterized by severe disturbances in thought, emotion and behaviour (324). Uncle Mahmoud asserts that Muftah's mental illness began after he witnessed his brother, Salah being blown up by a mine (73). The Italians had buried mines in Libya to demonstrate their distaste and spite for Libyans; hence is racial otherness. Correspondingly, Deeriye's religious insanity begins on the day Italians send a punitive expedition against him for defying their order to release the man who had killed an Italian administrator. They poison the cattle by contaminating the wells and shoot the remaining. The "painful mourning of cattle struggling with departing life" (41) confounds Deeriye so much that the ensuing depression compels him to pray incessantly. His psyche collapses and starts experiencing religious hallucinations. Farah writes:

> This was the first time Deeriye had crossed the known tactile world into one in which he could have visions, could hear prophecies, communicate with the beyond and reach out to and receive the guiding voices of other visionaries. (41)

The visionaries in this context refer to past sultans who exhort Deeriye to resist racial intimidation by the Italian military power. He hears a voice urging him "to persevere, hold to his principle" (42). It is therefore racial otherness that destroys Deeriye's psyche to pave way for his prophetic gift.

Whereas Matar does not express ethnic otherness in *The Return*, Farah in *Close Sesame* depicts suspicion between different Somali clans that tears the national fabric. In his study of Farah's *Close Sesame*, Hawley writes, "Farah returns again to his despair over Balkanizing effects of tribal patriotism within a new nation like Somalia," (196). The leadership divides the citizenry along ethnic lines to ensure its survival. Although clans, they are Somali ethnic groups because some differ in language and culture. The Italian colonial administration lays a foundation of ethnic otherness when it isolates those clans that resist from those that collaborate. When Deeriye rebels against the invaders' orders to appoint puppet chiefs, Italian administrators embrace Cigaal's clan and appoint chiefs from there. Henceforth the two clans exist in a state of tension. The conflict is evident when a madman called Khaliif starts cursing Cigaal's family. Yassin, a ten year old grandson of Cigaal picks stones to pelt him and Cigaal's family comes out to support the boy. Mursal, Deeriye's firstborn, comes out to support Khaliif by ordering the boy to drop the pebbles and leave, (21). We learn that Khaliif hails from Deeriye's clan whose resistance against oppression is as old as the advent of colonialism. When the Cigaal's are scared of Khaliif's recrimination and condemnation of the regime, Mursal intervenes to support his clansman.

Yassin's acts of violence embody the tension between Cigaal's and Deeriye's clan; it affects Deeriye such that he sees him in his hallucination. Yassin's pebbles signify otherness and this is why Deeriye is terribly frightened whenever he sees him (through the window) with the pebbles in hand. In a soliloquy, Deeriye says:

> You do not stone anybody: you cast stones at dogs, at madmen; you pelt an adulterous woman, say with stones, when at Mina in Mecca, you stone the pillar erected for that purpose. In the Islamic concept in which you take refuge when you curse the devil is the key-word 'rajiim' which defines Satan as the stoned one…nobody ever stones the object of one's love. (68)

In this text, Deeriye suggests that Cigaal's clan (through Yassin) views his clan as the devil represented by the pillar that is stoned my Muslims during the Haj at Mecca. To Cigaal's clan, Deereye's clan is just like dogs and adulteresses to be stoned by devout Muslims.

Ethnic otherness drives Khaliif to religious insanity possibly because he is tired of the evil in the General's regime. He hails from Deeriye's clan, which has been relegated since independence. Khaliif is one of the mad characters who in Robert Colson's view appropriates madness as mode of resistance by the oppressed clans against Somali dictatorship (i) because it is as a form of immunity to speak against tyranny. His love for Allah is unquestioned in his days of good health. He was meaningfully employed, with a family and car (16). His speeches reveal his love for the godly:

> There are wicked houses in which live wicked men and women. Truth must be owned up. We are God's children; the wicked of whom I speak are Satan's offspring. And night plots conspiracies daylight never reveals. (18)

Through him, the gods condemn corruption that manifests itself through betrayal, murder, falsehoods and other excesses of the regime. He exhorts those who love Allah to add more effort and decries the worship of human beings. Khaliif condemns social deviants that desecrate the cherished traditions of the land. He calls them "upstarts that upturn the sacred traditions and begin to worship men," (20). Khaliif is the god's mouthpiece in Deeriye's society in the manner in which he attracts huge crowds on the street. His criticism is without fear and favour as he attacks those within and without the clan. Deeriye and Mursal's silence after the demise of Mukhtaar stands out as a kind of betrayal and Mukhtaar launches an attack exhorting the faithful to curse Deeriye's family. He singles out Natasha, Mursal's Jewish wife as a foreign wife to be cursed and Deeriye and Mursal to be condemned for living with such a woman in the Muslim community (148). After the curses, Yassin, Cigaal's son is so happy with Khaliif that they shake hands (150). Yassin is now convinced that Khaliif does not just attack one clan but is evil and will there denounce anyone who commits it.

Conclusion

From the foregoing discussion, it indeed is unsatisfactory to view otherness as madness without a critical look at the root cause of it. Otherness is a cause of madness and if it is otherness then it brings itself into being. In other words, otherness is the cause of otherness and it is incumbent upon society to eradicate otherness to find any effective solution to the subsequent otherness, which is madness. It is also apparent that the dictator's psychopathic tendencies suggest their exposure to otherness during childhood.

Chapter Four
Otherness and Madness in African Drama

Introduction

The focus of the second chapter of this book was the link between othering conditions and the fragmented self in selected works of African drama. This chapter will interrogate the nexus between othering conditions and insanity. As much as the fragmented self has some symptoms similar to insanity, it is not the same as insanity. Hart associates madness with total alienation that results in the individual separating themselves completely from normal activities that human persons involve in (160). Whereas strains of the fragmented self can be as mild as depression, clinical madness is characterized by severe mental disturbance that is quite disabling. This section demonstrates how othering conditions results in severe mental disturbances in Francis Imbuga's Betrayal in the City, Ruganda's *Shreds of Tenderness* and Mulwa's *Inheritance*.

3.5 Political Otherness and Psychopathy in Three Works of Drama

Othering of groups politically has not just been demonstrated in prose fiction as explored in the previous subchapter. African playwrights such as David Mulwa, John Ruganda and Francis Imbuga have written extensively to show the nexus between political marginalisation and pathology. Whereas Ruganda and Mulwa's main focus is how instances of othering result in strains of the fragmented self, Imbuga is concerned with how political marginalization of groups leads to instances of clinical madness. This subsection takes Fanon's trajectory by focusing on the nexus between political othering, psychic collapse and total insanity (182) with reference to Imbuga's *Betrayal in the City*.

Set in a fictional African state, Kafira, *Imbuga's Betrayal in the City* is a tragicomedy of Jusper's determination to overthrow a tyrant. Few years after independence, a tyrant overthrows the government and introduces a highhanded regime that strips off the citizenry fundamental human rights and freedoms. While leading a peaceful demonstration, Adika, Jusper's elder brother, is shot in the cold blood. During the funeral, Adika's lecturer opposes restrictions imposed by the regime and he is arrested and detained without trial. Jere, a soldier who opposes, Mulili (the president's semi illiterate sycophant) is detained. In the prison, Mosese undergoes psychological disturbance as a result of the detention without trial. Jusper's mind disintegrates after his brother's demise and resolves to fight against the oppressive system, but by changing tact. He possibly points a finger of calumny at direct confrontation for Adika's death and opts for hybridity. Jusper joins the tyrant's inner circle in the pretext of supporting the regime. His entry into Boss's circle is spearheaded Tumbo's weaknesses. The most trusted of Boss's henchmen, Tumbo falls in love with Jusper's girlfriend, Regina and when they meet at her house, Jusper introduces himself as Regina's cousin. In attempt to bribe his prospective "brother in law," Tumbo transgresses procurement rules to give Jusper the task of writing a play to entertain a foreign dignitary. Jusper takes advantage to write a play in which Boss is one of the major characters. Deluded by the desire to please the dignitary, he allows prisoners to participate in the play, which gives detainees like Mosese and Jere a chance to participate in the play. During the dress rehearsal, Boss participates and naively allows actors to use real objects including live guns. At the climax of the play, the prisoners usurp the guns and threaten to shoot Boss. Jusper asks Boss' closest friend, Mulili why they should shoot Boss. Mulili betrays Boss saying that he should be killed because he is brutal, ruled for long and has destroyed the economy of Kafira. The play ends with the murder of Mulili and the spirits of Nina and Doga rejoicing.

Othering Conditions and Pathology: Schizophrenic Characters in the Three Selected Plays

> Francis Imbuga, a prolific Kenyan playwright [...] his long outstanding portrayal of his character's psyche through constant psychological motifs of madness, death and dreams. In an interview with Ahmad Harb, Imbuga admits that despite his plays being more obviously political, family or psychological subjects, they address themselves to the psyches of some of the major characters.
>
> *Roselyne Mutura*

Major characters in Imbuga's *Betrayal in the City* exhibit psychological problems that manifest through madness. In the above quote, Mutura underscores the manifestation of pathological conditions in Imbuga's characters through dreams and instances of madness. Whereas Mutura's focus is the "tripartite psyche" as the cause of madness in Imbuga's characters, this study contends that madness in these characters arises from the hostile political conditions. The chapter takes Imbuga's own trajectory when he asserts that his plays consider, "[t]he interaction of the conscious and unconscious mind of his lead characters and as such, dreams become very important in the understanding of his characters' unconscious," (Ahmed, 576). His reference to the conscious mind suggests the role of the cultural setting on the psyche of characters.

Boss, the villain of the play introduces in Kafira a system of governments that deprives the citizens' basic rights and freedoms. He suspends the constitutions and runs the country in an arbitrary way. He appoints a committee of sycophants that work for him under a strong spying network. Mulili, his henchman is a spy that checks the loyalty of all leaders and reports back to him. Given that he is illiterate, Mulili hastes intellectuals and invents crimes against them some of which are punishable by death. It is incredible how Boss trusts him to the point of killing noble men such as Kabito. A strait-laced and forthright member of the ruling elite, Kabito defends university students from being treated like children. He says this during the entertainment committee (planning reception of the dignitary) when Mulili says, "[w]hat we do, we do this: we ask for holiday, then every movable adult to line the road, not only the children," (55). An altercation ensues between Mulili and Kabito with the former accusing Kabito of vested interests because his son is a university student (56). As the chief spy in the autocratic regime, Mulili interprets what he hears according to his personal prejudices. When Kabito tells him to desist from treating university students as "primary kids," he blurts, "[w]ho you call primary kid?" (57). He then refuses to be dissuaded and orders Kabito to apologize like a person in absolute authority. When Kabito refuses, Mulili snarls, "[y]ou plays with fire you goat!" Boss and his henchmen have introduced in Kafira a regime in which the leader's thoughts cannot be challenged and anyone who contradicts them is perceived as the other.

Kabito therefore becomes the other after taking a contradicting stance against Mulili. After the short break that is given by Tumbo, Mulili goes to Boss's office and accuses him of tainting Boss' name and he orders his execution. When Mulili breaks the news of Kabito's death in a tragic road accident, Tumbo tells Nicodemo, "[s]omehow I felt it coming. Kabito should have known better than confront him," (62). Tumbo's suggestion reveals that Boss rules without expecting the slightest challenge or criticism. His government is a binary opposition to critics and either killed or detained without trial. Boss' style of leadership reiterates Richard Rorty's assertion on othering that "everything turns on who counts as a fellow human, as a rational agent in the only relevant sense-the sense in which rational agency is synonymous with membership of our moral community" (124). Those that do not think like Boss are not fellow human beings and that is why he imprisons or murders them. Tumbo summarizes the plight of characters under Boss' othering regime as "like caged animals, we move, but only inside the cage," (62). All the citizens of Kafira belong to the outgroup and can lose their lives anytime. They are subjected to stringent rules and those who disagree are terribly punished. Tumbo reveals to Jusper that when Boss loses temper, "he can hardly tell a human being from a rat," (65). This assertion demonstrates aspects of othering as explicated by Rorty. Boss looks at people that oppose him as nonhumans.

In a conversation with Jusper before the dress rehearsal, Boss demonstrates his distaste for those people he considers "others." He blurts:

> Represent the intellectuals well. (*seriously*). Some of the reports I get from there are simply disgusting. Who made you students spokesmen of truth and justice?
> Jusper: Nothing, Your Excellency
> Boss: Completely nothing [...] when you go back, tell their leaders that it is my duty to decide on the magnitude of Kafira's Africanization programme. They have no right to chant about it. (67)

Boss creates the binary typical of othering by claiming that as a self, he solely possesses the means to superintend the Africanization of Kafira. All his critics are foolish and without a blue print to the direction Kafira will take. His thinking reiterates Levi Strauss' contention that "people will use expletives like 'barbarous habits', 'ought not to be allowed, not what we do' to reject any moral, religious, social ideas, which differ from what they know (11). In league with Strauss' maxim, Boss critics such as Jusper, Mosese, Jere and university students are therefore foolish because they have anti despotic ideas that differ from his. In the conversation, Boss brags of how he has harmed the *other*: "a dead student leader and senior lecturer in prison" (67). This is a reference to Adika, the chair of the student council of the University of Kafira who leads a strike to oppose the influx of expatriates in the country. Although it is a peaceful demonstration, Boss' regime otherizes these students because of their divergent "social ideas" as Strauss suggests. He sends police officers that brutally attack them. Adika's father, Doga says: "[t]here were many of them, all marching in the same manner. Suddenly, the shooting broke out. People fled in all directions, but my son's lonely body lay in the middle of the street. Only four bullets were fired that day. Adika had four bullet wounds on his chest," (4). Doga makes it clear in this passage that Adika was the target of police onslaught. Jusper, Adika's young brother is so traumatized by Adika's death that he takes revenge by killing the police officer who shot Adika.

The dictatorial regime extends its othering tactics to Adika's funeral by instituting stringent rules on the people attending the funeral. In a conversation between Jere and Mosese, the latter says:

> A handful politicians tried to turn the funeral service into a political rally. The service must not take more than ten minutes. The coffin should not be carried by students. Weeping in public is illegal for the academic staff. I couldn't bear it, so I told them my mind. The following day they came for me. (25)

This passage reveals Boss' resolve to deny the other attributes of humanity as suggested by Rorty and Strauss. Fanon observes that political and racial othering entails denying the other attributes of humanity that possibly results in psychic collapse (1961, 182). Because Adika's relatives and friends do not share Boss' political ideology (autocracy), their burial service must be brief, and his teacher should not cry. The students should not carry the corpse. Mosese, one of Adika's lectures defies the orders; he is arrested and detained without trial. Jere, the soldier who is sent to stop the shaving ceremony is detained after sympathizing with Doga and Nina and allowing them to carry on with it. Boss then sends his henchmen to kill the two such that when Jusper is released from detention, he comes back to an empty home.

As a result of political othering characters' psyches take Fanon's trajectory by exhibiting symptoms of madness. Jusper's mental illness begins after receiving the news of Adika's death. The news is so traumatizing that as Fanon suggests Jusper's psyche collapses; Doga observes that upon receiving the news, "Jusper was never the same again. He became wild at the funeral, singing songs of vengeance," (4). He was taken away and is possibly tortured because when he returns, Doga says, "he was no longer the son we knew" (5). Jusper exhibits symptoms of schizophrenia, which Davison defines as a mental disorder characterized by severe disturbances in thought, emotion and behaviour. The person's thinking is illogical, perception, faulty accompanied with inappropriate affect and disturbances in motor activity (324). John Csernansky refers to acute schizophrenic phase as psychosis (109). Jusper's speech demonstrates severe thought disturbance for instance he says:

> Hey, come to think of it! You and I have never seen, Jupiter, except...? Except on paper. *Jupiter? - Absent sir. Jusper, present sir. Jusper! Absent sin yes* I've got it. Jupiter and justice are one and the same. They are neither here and there [...] squad, attention, aim...one, two, three, two, one, fire! Tutututututu! Squad! Squad, attention! Hey, sergeant, why, why you looking sad eeh? (5-6)

This conversation demonstrates the illogical thought and severe mental disturbance because particularly when he says Jupiter is absent and Jusper is absent sin. The last part of the conversation entails nonsensical expressions that are symptomatic of schizophrenia. His suggestion that Justice is as absent as Jupiter is a truth that Michel Foucault singles out as the invaluable attribute of madness in literature. He writes:

> By the madness which interrupts it, a work of art opens a void, a moment of silence, a question, a question without answer, provokes a breach without reconciliation where the world is forced to question itself [...] the world is made aware of its guilt. Through the mediation of madness, it is the world that becomes culpable in relation to the work. (286)

The work of art therefore needs madness to express its ideas more effectively and so creative writers like Imbuga cannot ignore madness in their desire to reveal certain truths about effects of political othering. Going by Foucault perspective, Imbuga creates a mad character to express sensitive truths.

Mosese is another character whose psyche collapses because of the political othering in Kafira. In prison Jere is shocked to see him wake up and walks around. This sleepwalking is a psychological condition that has arisen from political persecution by Boss. In the stage directions, the playwright says:

> Suddenly, Mosese utters a terrible war-cry. He wriggles violently as if in a fight and then stops suddenly. Now he stands up slowly as if in slow motion picture. His eyes are wide open and unblinking. He walks around cell greeting old friends and relatives. Jere now frightened, edges against the wall. (30)

Mosese's sleep walking is followed by Mosese's communication to people Jere cannot see. He says, "I suppose I will marry, yes…That was inevitable…Thank you. I am glad you think so," (31). Hart refers to such experiences as hallucinations, defined as false sense impressions or sensory experiences in the absence of any stimulation from the environment (48). Jere concludes that Mosese's insanity is derived from the political situation in Kafira. He says, "[w]hen the madness of an entire nation disturbs a solitary mind, it is not enough to say that the man is mad," (31). Unlike Mutura's argument that madness arises from characters' mental orientation, Imbuga in Jere's assertion suggests that the political condition of Kafira is the major cause of clinical madness in characters.

Similarly, clinical madness is evident in Ruganda's *Shreds of tenderness* and Mulwa's *Inheritance*. In Ruganda's play, Odie has severe psychological disturbances and has been in and out of the penitentiary. As the play begins, Stella advises him to pay another visit to the psychiatrist saying, "I think the malady is back," (11). She advises him to visit Dr Kyambadde for a check-up (28), Odie gets infuriated and hurls insults at Stella, but his preoccupations exhibit the idleness and oddity typical of clinical madness. Odie enters the dining hall:

> Carrying a large glass jar in the armpits, a couple of ice trays in one hand and a Bunsen burner in the other. He places them in the end of the table. The glass jar is in the centre...he re-enters carrying another jar, an ice container and a tin of pesticide which he is playing with in imitation of the guns. He places everything on the table, arranges them to suit his purpose before he sits down. Persistently tapping the central jar, he addresses the jar between the tappings. (2)

Throughout this scene at the opening of the play, Odie is absolutely disinterested in Stella and is engrossed in meaningless experiments and apostrophes. In the ensuing address, he talks to the King of termites calling him "his highness" and at some instances, breaking down. He claims that he will use the Bunsen burner to torture all opponents of the king. Davison singles out avolition as a symptom of clinical madness in which the patient spends much time idling around (329). Odie spends a good proportion of the day shouting at the jar until Stella asks him, "[w]hy waste so much time? Haven't you have something better to do?" (10) Odie also exhibits delusions, which Davison defines as false beliefs their close allies are working in cahoots with their persecutors to harm them (327). Odie believes that even Stella his only sister is working with Wak to destroy him. Odie's poverty of relationships is asociability, which Goldberg and Schimidt defines as severely impaired social relationships among schizophrenics. In his family, he maintains hostile relationships with his father, stepbrother Wak and Sister Stella. Of his late father, he says, "[r]egarded me a failure. An embarrassment to the family," (30) and goes ahead to betray him to his enemies. Witu is detained and assassinated after Odie informs on him. He lives with this guilty, which eats into his self such that he consistently pleads with him through apostrophes. In the presence of Wak, Odie says to the late father, "Go away, Papa. Leave me alone. I did not kill your cow with a catapult," (129). This plea is followed with an utterance that confirms that Odie has not forgiven his late father. He still hates him because he said, "[y]ou are a perfect replica of your mother's IQ" (129). Odie also hates his brother, Wak and reacts with shocking distaste when Stella says he has returned. He blurts out, "he should be shot" (13). To Stella, his own blood sister, he snarls, "[y]ou were a perfect circus for an audience of octopuses, you dabbling your eyes like a trachoma case and him sniffing away like a dog in the cold winds of winter (23). Odie says this with reference to Stella's loving relationship with Wak. He harps on his affair with Mohamed Ali to justify his meanness towards Wak. As much as he claims that they are all dehumanized by war, the insistence on the affair is a betrayal of Stella. Odie is therefore disinterested in other human beings and at forty-four, he has not shown any interest in the opposite sex. Davison refers to this as achedonia, a nother clinical symptom of schizophrenia (329). Wak opines, "[i]t is high time you got married, man. Might help you get over your hatred of everything decent," (121). Patients with achedonia completely fail to nurture "close relationships with other people and lack interest in sex" (Davison, 329).

Finally Odie's speech demonstrates clinical madness with regard to incoherence. Davison points out disorganized speech as a main symptom of schizophrenia. Most of the answers he gives are not connected to the questions asked. When Wak reads from Odies SRB file concerning "pockets of insurgence" that Odie had reported, he replies, "[t]he tick starts with the block, the termite with the base" (127). The answer given is absolutely irrelevant to the question Wak asks. The playwright leads the reader to Odie's insanity at the beginning of the answer by the statement, "his mind trailing" (127). Odie then trails further into nonsensical, "the river roaring like a pack of lines. Can you hear me, Tickie?" (128) Wak asks Odie again what he meant by writing, "[t]he dog will be deported and Daudi detained," and he replies, "[c]ows, class and cowardice. Killed the cow and flunked in class," (128). Davison asserts that disorganized speech emanates from mind's inability to organize ideas so that people can understand.

Madness in Mulwa's *inheritance* is exhibited in the character Lacuna and Tamina respectively. Although he belongs to the dominant group, Lacuna's behaviour demonstrates clinical madness through clinical symptoms such as asociability, apostrophes and delusions. Like Odie in Shreds of tenderness, Lacuna has hostile relationship with his father. Deceived by his father's enemies, he kills him using poison and lives with constant guilty throughout his life. He says of his father, "[h]e loved me Daniel and I killed him" (69). Lacuna also hates his wife Melisa. When the girl he has designs on reminds him that she loves his wife Melisa, he snarls, "[w]ife! A demon! A tongue of living lightning! An oversize matchstick of angry dynamite!" (94). Lacuna hates the closest person he should love the most. He does not love his adoptive sister, Sangoi. When she advises him about the need to appease the ancestors, he retorts, "I forgot you used to prattle with him in his makeshift court," (56). Later, he appoints her a minister without any bodyguards. Lacuna cannot maintain any close relationships even with Robert and Goldstein who finance his budget. Goldstein is so close that he advises him to kill the father. When they question his misappropriation of funds, he blurts, "[...]we are a sovereign state! Can't be dictated to by a boy smarting from initiation!" (82). He detains them even against the will of his spiritual advisers. He insists on having sex with Lulu, which is contrary to tradition. When the spiritual advisors insist, he breaks ranks with them describing them as "[n]ational witchdoctor," (116). He declares himself a god and as the revolution gathers to dethrone him, he calls the people "mass of illiterate people" with no knowledge of international business (86). When he is advised that the people are up in arms against him, he gives a shocking reply that all the people are with him. Later, the truth dawns on him that he has no intimate relationship with any one and descends into apostrophes. Davison refers to this oddity as bizarre behaviour in which schizophrenics start talking to themselves (330). In one instance, Lacuna orders Chipande to summon Lulu in his presence and then speaks:

> My father, lay not my sin across my doorstep and let your son serve your children for yet another term. (*he kneels*). See only humility upon my bended knee. See only penitence and let the bridge stay in place....only this once and I shall. (89)

The bridge Lacuna refers to in the extract refers to his father's curse before he gave up his ghost. After taking the poison, he tells Lacuna that when the flood rises against him to destroy the bridge then Lacuna's reign would have reached its end. The flood signifies the revolution that Bengo and Sangoi spearhead to dethrone Lacuna's corrupt regime. These apostrophes recur severally to demonstrate Lacuna's schizophrenic tendencies. In a conversation with Goldstein about his inheritance, Lacuna descends into another apostrophe:

> My father likes sugar…his weakness…I have brought you your favourite tea, my father." And he's that smile!...he's blessing me…that childlike , trusting heart. 'my dutiful son!" he loves me and I am about to…' (68)

Goldstein who witnesses this scene is confounded at the confession, which should be Lacuna's top secret. The constant reference to the father suggests that like Odie, Lacuna's condition stems from age othering. His father is so busy to look after him and proceeds to prepare Sangoi, the adoptive sister as the heir to the throne. Taking advantage of the situation, neo-colonialists incite him to kill his own father. Lacuna is therefore a victim of otherness at the family level.

Lastly, Tamina is so much oppressed by the lacuna regime until she loses her sanity. Her predicament starts when her husband Judah Zen Melo refuses to kill his brother Bengo in defiance of Lacuna's request (23). He is sacked, tortured and left for dead (23). Their land is given to Chipande and they descend into abject poverty. To possess their daughter, Lulu, Lacuna sends hitmen to kill Zen Melo at the mines. When Tamina receives, the news, her self starts the process of disintegration. She experiences hallucinations and out of body experience. She tells onlooker:

> I can't reach the coffee beans…my body…as if chewed by a leopard and can't get it together again. Help me. I'm drifting apart. Help me someone […] I'm rolling home…eternity…and I'm sitting here, finally, and then I see him in my dream and he's smiling at me: "I'm coming home! Look I'm strong now…see how I glow with strength and happiness. (99-100)

At the beginning of this excerpt Tamina's self is separated from her body and it starts encountering her husband's spiritual self, which onlookers such as Sangoi cannot see. Hart asserts that in hallucinations, the schizophrenic sees an "object that has no real existence" (48). In her speech after overthrowing Lacuna, Sangoi says about Tamina, "[w]e all know the story of this mother, Tamina Zen Melo, and others like her. Since disaster struck her home, she has lost her mind," (134-135). The "disaster" Sangoi refers to are the othering conditions Tamina experiences after her husband disagrees with Lacuna. They become the Other because they do not think like Lacuna and the ensuing acts of repression destroy her psyche.

Conclusion

Strands of othering do not just cause fragmentation of the selves in characters but result in severe psychological disturbances. As much as Odie experiences self-alienation in Ruganda's *Shreds of tenderness*, there are many instances in his life that demonstrate that he is a victim of schizophrenia. From the experiments at the start of the play to the disorganized speeches, Odie's behaviour gives evidence to justify his visits to the psychiatrist. Similarly, Mosese and Jusper's odd behaviour confirm the presence of clinical madness arising from political othering. As much as Odie and Lacuna belong to the dominant group, the writers suggests that most dictators were victims of age othering during childhood. It is also possible that the dominant group has to lose their sanity to turn the marginal group to insanity.

Chapter Five

SUMMARY AND CONCLUSIONS

This book set forth to interrogate the nexus between culture and madness in selected works of African prose and drama. The study is drawn from the conversation that constant attempts to focus of the individual patient in the treatment of madness without consideration of cultural context is absurd. The study is based on the Fanon's assertion that colonialist racist theories informed the callousness with which colonialism was executed to "disrupt the cultural life" of the colonized through "negation of national reality…banishment of natives and their customs," (235) which dented the self-esteem of the colonized. In the last chapter of *The Wretched of the Earth*, "The Colonial War and Mental Disorders," Fanon summarises his views on colonialism as, "[a] systematised negation of the other, a frenzied attempt to deny the other any attribute of humanity…which if left unchallenged by armed resistance, the colonized's defenses collapse and many of them end up in psychiatric institutions," (250). Fanon adds that a stream of symptoms of madness ensues as "sequels of the oppression" (250). It is upon this argument that this study set off to analyse the nexus between strands of othering and psychological anomalies in selected works of African prose fiction and drama.

The first chapter focused on the nexus between strands of othering such as racial and political othering and the fragmented self. The chapter focused on selected works of prose fiction such as Alex La Guma's *A Walk in the Night*, Wanner's *London, Cape*

Town, Joburg, Farah's *Close Sesame* and Matar's *The Return*. It was discovered that most characters in these novels were victims of diverse strands of the fragmented self such as the shattered self, the non-self, depression and asexuality owing to the othering conditions they live in. Characters such as Michael Adonis and Uncle Dougthy in La Guma's *A Walk in the Night* are driven to alcoholism because of the political and racial othering in apartheid South Africa. It was interesting to note that some strains of the fragmented self cause suicide and asexuality in Farah's *Close Sesame*.

The second chapter turns away from the fragmented self in prose fiction to African drama with reference to the works of Ruganda's *Shreds of Tenderness* and Mulwa's *Inheritance*. One prevalent strand of the fragmented self in the play was the under stimulated self that exhibits itself through sexual perversions and alcoholism. Judah Zen Melo is driven and Odie in *Inheritance* and *Shreds of Tenderness* respectively affected by the political othering to self-alienation and alcohol addiction. Age othering stands out as one of the causes of the fragmented self with reference to Ruganda's play *Shreds of Tenderness*. Narcissistic personality disorder was identified as an aspect of the fragmented self that stems from age othering in Mulwa's *Inheritance*.

Chapter three focused on the nexus between othering conditions and madness in prose fiction with reference to Farah's *Close sesame*, *Gifts* and Matar's *The Return*. Political, racial and gender othering distinguished themselves as causes of schizophrenia in characters such as Muftah in Matar's *The Return* and Mukhtaar in *Close Sesame*.

The focus of Chapter Four was the nexus between othering and madness in African drama with reference to Imbuga's *Betrayal in the city*, Ruganda's *Shreds of Tenderness* and Mulwa's *Inheritance*. The chapter overturned conversations that negate the cultural environment in the study of madness in literary characters. It was discovered that psychological anomalies in characters such as

Tamina, Odie, Jusper and Mosese in the three plays arise from age and political othering rather than their unconscious. It was insightful to note that even characters that are related to the dominant group such as Odie and Lacuna exhibit symptoms of madness.

Works Cited

Abdi, Safi. *A Mighty Collision of Two Worlds*. Bloomington: Authorhouse, 2002.

Adorn, Theodore, Frenkel Brunswk, Daniel Levinson and Nevitt Sanford. *The Authoritarian Personality*. Herper and Row, 1950.

Amhad, Harb. "The Aesthetics of Francis Imbuga: A Contemporary Kenyan Playwright." *Literary Review*, vol. 34, no. 4, summer 1991, pp. 571. Web. 21, January, 2016.

Anderson, Jon. *Understanding Cultural Geography Places and Traces*. Routledge, 2009.

Antony, Martin. "Anxiety Disorders: Social and Specific Phobias". *Psychiatry*. Eds. A. Tasman, J. Kay and J.A Lieberrman. New York: John Wiley and Sons, 2003. 1298-1330.

Ashcroft, Bill, Gareth Griffiths and Hellen Tiffin, eds. *Postcolonial Studies Reader*. London: Routledge, 1995

Breidlid, Anders. "Resistance and Consciousness in Kenya and South Africa: A Comparative Study with Particular Reference to the Novels of Ngugi wa Thiong'o and Alex La Guma." University of London, 2001.

Bootzin, Richard & Acocella Joan. *Abnormal Psychology: Current Perspectives* 5th Ed. New York. Random House, 1972.

Canales, M. K. "Othering: Difference Understood? A Ten Year Analysis and Critique of the Nursing Literature." *Advances in Nursing Science*, 33 (2010): 15-34.

Caputo, John. "Forget Rationality is There Religious Truth?" *Madness Religion and the Limits of Reason*. Eds. Jonna Bornemark and Sven-Olov Wallenstein. Huddinge: Sodertorn University, 2015. Pp. 23-41.

Csernansky, John. *Schizophrenia: A New Gude for Clinicians*. New York: Mercel and Dekker, 2002.

Cornel. Gareth. "Style is the Great 'Betrayer': Socialist Realism in La Guma's *A Walk in the Night*". *English Studies in Africa* 54.1 (2011): 11- 20.

Chigwedere, Yuleth. "Head of Darkness: Representations of Madness in Postcolonial Zimbabwean Literature." University of South Africa, 2015.

Chikwava, Brian. *Harare North*. London: Vintage Books, 2009

Chiweshe, Manase. "Wives at Market Place: Commercialisation of Lobola and Commodification of Women's Bodies in Zimbabwe." *The Oriental Anthropologist*, 16. 2 (2016): 229-243.

Clingman, Stephen. *The Grammar of Identity: Transnational Fiction and the Nature of the Boundary*. Oxford: OUP, 2009.

Colson, Robert. "The Performance of Madness as Resistance in Nuruddin Farah's *Close Sesame."* *Ariel* 46.4 (2015):10-35

Cooke, Rachel. "The Return by Hisham Matar- Exquisite Pain of a Fatherless Son." The Guardian. 2016. https://www.theguardian.com/books/2016/jul/03/.

Cousineau, Tara and Domar Alice. "Psychological Impact of Infertility". *Best Practices and Research in Clinical Obsterics and Gynaecology*, 21. 2 (2007): 293-308.

Davison, Gerald. *Abnormal Psychology*. Ontario: John Wiley & Sons, 2008.

Derrida, Jacques. "Circumfession. Fifty- Nine Periods and Periphrases." *Jacques Derrida translated by Geofrey Bennington*. University of Chicago Press, 1993.

Downs, Anthony. "An Economic Theory of Political Action in a Democracy." *Journal of Political Economy*, 65. 2 (1957): 135-150.

Fanon, Frantz. *The Wreched of the Earth with Commentary by Jean Paul and Homi K. Bhabha*.Trans. Richard Philcox. New York. Groove Press, 1961.

Farah, Nurudin. *Close Sesame*. Allison and Busby Ltd, 1983

Feder, Lillian. *Madness in Literature*. Princeton University Press,

1980.

Focault, Michel. *Madness and Civilization*. Roultedge Classics, 1961.

Goldberg, J., O. and Schimidt, L., A. "Shyness, Sociability and Social Function in Schizophrenia". *Schizophrenia Research*, 48: Pp. 343-349.

Goldin, Ian. "The Reconstitution of Colored Identity in Western Cape." *The Politics of Race, Class and Nationalism in the Twentieth Century South Africa*. Eds. Shule Marks and Stanley Trapicle. London and New York: Longman, 1987. P. 170.

Gray, R.,Gross, R., Goebel R. & Koelb, C. *A Frantz Kafka Encyclopaedia*. Westport: Greenswood Press, 2005.

Hall, Stuart. "Cultural Identity and Diaspora." Rutherford, Jonathan. *Identity, Culture, Difference*. Lawrence and Wishart, 1990.

Hart, Bernard. *The Psychology of Insanity*. New York. The Macmillan Company, 1931.

Hawley, John. "Mourning and melancholy in Hisham Matar's *In the Country of Men* and *Anatomy of Disapperance*." Santa Clara University, 2017.

Hegel, George. *The Phenology of the Mind*, trans. J.B. Baille. Harper & Row Publishers, 1967.

Kramatschek, Claudia. "A Painful Void: Book Review of Matar's *The Return*." Qantara.de. 2017. https://en.qantara.de/content/book-review-hisham-matars-the-return-a-painful-void.

Kohut Heinz and Wolf Ernest. "Disorders of the Self and their Treatment: An Outline." *The International Journal of Psychoanalysis* 59 (1978): 413-425.

La Guma, Alex. *A walk in the Night and Other Stories*. Illnois. North Western university Press, 1968. 56-65.

Laing D. Ronald. *The Divided Self: An Existential Study of Sanity and Madness*. Penguin, 1960.

Malone, Andrew. "God the Illeist: Third Person Self-References and Trinitarian Hints in the Old Testament." *JETS* 52.3 (2014): 499-518. www.etsjets.org/files. Web. 29th July 2019.

Lindstrom, Anders. "Divine Frenzy and the Poetics of Madness". Eds. Jonna Bornemark and Sven- Olov Wallenstein. *Madness, Religion and the Limits of Reason.* Huddinge: Sodertorn University, 2015. 53-74.

Matar, Hisham. *The Return.* Penguin Books, 2017.

Mellor C. S. "First Rank Symptoms of Schizophrenia." *British Journal of Psychiatry,* 117: 15-23.

Mkhize, Jabulani. "Social Realism and Alex La Guma's Longer Fiction." University of Natal, 1998.

Mnthali, Felix. "Autocracy and the Limits of Identity: A Reading the Novels of Nuruddin Farah." *Ufahamu: A Journal of African Studies* 17. 2 (1989): 53-60. www.escholarship.org/uc/item/shgygwn.

Moolla, F. Fatima. "Individualism in the Novels of Nuruddin Farah." *Corpus.* 2009. https://www.open.uct.ac.za

Mutura, Roselyne. "The Tripartite Psyche as Reflection of Social Vision in Selected Plays of Francis Imbuga," 2019 MA Dissertation Kenyatta University.

Ngema, Nqobizwe. "Polygamy Versus Equality Rights: Is Polyandry a Solution." *International Journal of Sustainable Development.* 9. 7(2016): p. 11- 14.

Okasha, A. and Okasha, T. 2012. " Religion, Spirituality and the Cocept of Mental Illness. *Actasesp Psiquaia* 40 (2): 73-79.

Reid, Gregory. *A Reexamination of Tragedy and Madness in Eight Selected Plays from the Greeks to the 20th Century,* Lewiston: Mellen, 2002.

Roberts, Donald. "Madness and Culture: A Study of Madness in the Works of Woolf, Chekov and Fitzgerald," Simon Fraser University, 1980. www.pdfs.semantischolar.org.

Showalter, Elaine. *Sexual Anarchy: Gender and Culture at the Fin de*

*Siecle.*London: Bloomsbury, 1991.
Satre, Jean-Paul & Arlette Elkaime-Satre. *Existentialism is Humanism.* Yale University Press, 2007.
Shihada, Isam. "The Patriarchal Class System in Nawal El Saadawi's God Dies by the Nile." *Nebula.* 42 (2007): 162-182.
Snow, Kim. "Vulnerable Citizens: The Oppression of Children in Care". *Journal of child and youth care work,* 21 (2009):Pp. 94-113.
Strauss, Levi. *Trites Tropiques.* Penguin, 1955, 1992.
Walsh, Ben. *Modern World History.* Hodder Murray, 1996.
Williams P. Heather. "South African Homes: The Spatial Politics of Belonging in Post-Apartheid Novels." Ph.D Diss. The University of Tennesse, 2017. https://trace.tennesse.edu/utk-groddiss/4783.
Zeleza, T. Paul. "Visions of Freedom and Democracy in Postcolonial African Literature." *Women's Studies Quarterly* 25.3 (1997): 10-34. www.jstor.org/stable/40003370.

Mmap Nonfiction and Academic books

If you have enjoyed **Otherness and Pathology: The Fragmented Self and Madness in Contemporary African Fiction**, consider these other fine *Nonfiction and Academic* books from Mwanaka Media and Publishing:

Cultural Hybridity and Fixity by Andrew Nyongesa
Tintinnabulation of Literary Theory by Andrew Nyongesa
South Africa and United Nations Peacekeeping Offensive Operations by Antonio Garcia
A Case of Love and Hate by Chenjerai Mhondera
A Cat and Mouse Affair by Bruno Shora
The Scholarship Girl by Abigail George
The Gods Sleep Through It All by Wonder Guchu
PHENOMENOLOGY OF DECOLONIZING THE UNIVERSITY: *Essays in the Contemporary Thoughts of Afrikology by Zvikomborero Kapuya*
Africanization and Americanization Anthology Volume 1, Searching for Interracial, Interstitial, Intersectional and Interstates Meeting Spaces, Africa Vs North America by Tendai R Mwanaka
Africa, UK and Ireland: Writing Politics and Knowledge Production Vol 1 by Tendai R Mwanaka
Writing Language, Culture and Development, Africa Vs Asia Vol 1 by Tendai R Mwanaka, Wanjohi wa Makokha and Upal Deb
Zimbolicious: An Anthology of Zimbabwean Literature and Arts, Vol 3 by Tendai Mwanaka
Drawing Without Licence by Tendai R Mwanaka
Writing Grandmothers/ Escribiendo sobre nuestras raíces: Africa Vs Latin America Vol 2 by Tendai R Mwanaka and Felix Rodriguez

Nationalism: (Mis)Understanding Donald Trump's Capitalism, Racism, Global Politics, International Trade and Media Wars, Africa Vs North America Vol 2 by Tendai R Mwanaka
It Is Not About Me: Diaries 2010-2011 by Tendai Rinos Mwanaka
Chitungwiza Mushamukuru: An Anthology from Zimbabwe's Biggest Ghetto Town by Tendai Rinos Mwanaka
The Day and the Dweller: A Study of the Emerald Tablets by Jonathan Thompson
Zimbolicious Anthology Vol 4: An Anthology of Zimbabwean Literature and Arts by Tendai Rinos Mwanaka and Jabulani Mzinyathi
Parks and Recreation by Abigail George
FAMILY LAW AND POLITICS WITH BIOLOGY AND ROYALTY IN AFRICA AND NORTH AMERICA by Peter Ateh-Afec Fossungo
Writing Robotics, Africa Vs Asia, Vol 2 by Tendai Rinos Mwanaka
Zimbolicious Anthology Vol 5: An Anthology of Zimbabwean Literature and Arts by Tendai R. Mwanaka
Love Notes: Everything is Love, An Anthology of Indigenous Languages of Africa and East Europe by Tendai R Mwanaka
Zimbabwe: Beyond Robert Mugabe by Tendai Rinos Mwanaka
Zimbolicious Anthology Vol 6: An Anthology of Zimbabwean Literature and Arts by Tendai R. Mwanaka and Chenjerai Mhondera
BATTLING LANGUAGE RIGHTS GOVERNANCE IN AFRICA: SWISSELGIANISM, UBACKISM, AND THE AMBAZONIA-CAMEROUN WAR by Peter Ateh-Afec Fossungo

https://facebook.com/MwanakaMediaAndPublishing/

www.ingramcontent.com/pod-product-compliance
Lightning Source LLC
Chambersburg PA
CBHW010832230426